# CHRISTMAS
## On Parade

### 18 fast & easy wall quilts to celebrate the season

Marie Shirer & Marla Stefanelli

Leman
Quilt Books

# Introduction

Christmas is a time for stories. Beginning with the Bible story of the Nativity, Mary and Joseph travel to the little town of Bethlehem where Jesus is born. About that same time, an angel appears to shepherds, who are watching their flocks by night, to tell them the great news. Soon thereafter, three kings are advised to follow a star and see for themselves what has happened.

This story is just the beginning of countless Christmas traditions. For many people, Santa Claus is now the central character in a host of holiday stories. Santa is such a personable fellow that it's only natural that he would have a wife and some elves to help him with his important work.

Rudolph the red-nosed reindeer–known to his close friends as Rudy–has now become more famous than the original eight reindeer. And we couldn't have holiday prime-time television without the favorite cartoon featuring Frosty the Snowman.

If you're someone whose favorite Christmas stories include classical music and ballet, surely you are well aware of the story of the Nutcracker and the Sugar Plum Fairy.

All of these Christmas characters parade through this book of 18 wall quilts. Rounding out the characters you will find bells, Christmas trees and stars to remind us of the sounds, smells and lights of the season.

Interwoven with the traditional stories of Christmas are cherished family tales of celebrating this most wonderful time of the year. Many quiltmakers add to their family's traditions by making special quilts that are displayed or used only a few weeks out of the year. Then they are tucked away with other holiday treasures to be loved and cherished again the next year.

We hope the projects in this book offer you plenty of variety to emphasize your favorite Christmas traditions. Perhaps the Nativity figures are central to your celebration. Or maybe Santa and his team are the key to a magical holiday. Of course you can mix and match them to your heart's content. Introduce the three kings to Pixie and Tinker the Elves and see what happens!

Two of the projects deserve a special mention because they are perfect for year-'round celebrating. The Nutcracker is also a toy soldier for your special little guy, and the Sugar Plum Fairy is a lovely ballerina for a little girl's room. Just as Tchaikovsky's music "The Nutcracker Suite" is heard year 'round, children can enjoy these special playmates 12 months of the year.

So create your own special Christmas story with these quilts that are all fast and easy. They are designed so you can actually complete them before the holidays. All you need are a few hours (really!), a little fabric, perhaps a few buttons and bells, and you will be on your way.

Happy holidays!

*Marie and Marla*

# Contents

# Special Techniques

The quilts in this book have been designed to use several special techniques that are not only easy and quick, but a lot of fun as well. These special methods are explained here, at the beginning of the book, so you can read about them before starting your projects. However, at the back of the book, on pages 56-60, you will also find General Instructions for all the basic techniques used to make these quilts. The information covered there includes sizing, selecting fabrics, cutting patches, piecing, appliqué, adding borders and corner squares, assembling the layers and quilting, adding tabs and binding the quilt, and making a label. If you are a beginning quilter, be sure to read that section (as well as this one) to find a lot of helpful instruction. If you have made quilts before, you might want to use that section mainly for reference when questions arise.

## 3-D Piecing

This technique gives extra dimension for areas such as hair bangs (Shepherd, Mary, Heavenly Angel, Mrs. Claus, Tinker the Elf, Sugar Plum Fairy, King II), trims (Joyful Bells, Santa's hat, Frosty's hat), the brim on the Nutcracker's hat, and the "hanging" parts of Frosty's scarf and Tinker the Elf's hat. Patches that are 3-D pieced have a double layer of fabric.

Each set of project directions will tell you which patches to use for 3-D piecing and how to sew them. Patches are cut and folded

with wrong sides together or are sewn before being basted to other patches. For example, several projects have triangles of hair that are 3-D pieced over a square face. Simply follow the directions to add the 3-D patches before piecing the quilt top. The basted edges will be caught in the seams.

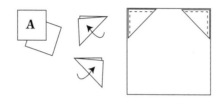

For the Sugar Plum Fairy and Mary, the hair bangs are cut from a rectangle of fabric that is folded in half lengthwise. Project directions will show you how to place the folded fabric to create the desired angle. After basting, trim the edges of the folded strip so that the hair patch matches the shape of the face.

Some patches will need to be sewn to make the 3-D patch. The brim on the Nutcracker's hat and Rudy the Reindeer's ears are done this way. Just follow project patterns and directions to sew these pieces right sides together. Turn them right side out, press, and baste them in place before piecing the quilt top.

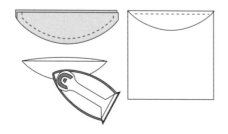

## 3-D Appliqué

This technique is similar to 3-D piecing, except that appliqués are made with a double layer of fabric and are sewn to the quilt after it is quilted and bound. Examples of projects where 3-D appliqué can be used include large mustaches, Frosty's flower and the star flowers on Starry Night. All patches that can be done in 3-D appliqué can also be done with traditional hand appliqué. The quilts shown use both techniques.

To make 3-D appliqués, cut patches that include ¼" seam allowances. Sew two patches with right sides together. Clip inner curves of seams and trim seam allowances on points. Cut a small slit (about 1" long) in the patch that will be the back side. Cut carefully to be sure only one layer of fabric is slit. Turn appliqué right side out through the slit. Use a pin or needle to gently pull the seam to form a smooth edge; press flat.

3-D appliqués are sewn in place after the quilting and binding are finished. To attach 3-D appliqués, pin them in place with the slit side touching the quilt. Working from the back side of the quilt, take a few hand stitches through all layers of the quilt to hold the appliqué in place. Some

3-D appliqués, such as the flower stars on Starry Night, will be sewn in place with a button on top. It's a good idea to use thread that matches the appliqué or button (not the quilt lining) so stitches will not be noticeable on the front of the quilt.

# Embellishments

There are no limits to the kind and amount of embellishments you can use on these quilts. Feel free to use any or all of the options given here and in the project directions, but also add other objects, trims and techniques as you wish.

Embellishments for these quilts can be divided into two categories: those that are added as the quilt top is made and before it is quilted, and those that are added after the quilting and binding are finished. The difference is that the first category has techniques and items that are flat and therefore will not interfere with the quilting. The second category has techniques and objects that are bulkier and therefore could interfere with the quilting.

## Those Added Before Quilting

**Embroidery:** Several of the quilts use embroidery for face details, and you can choose any colors that appeal to you for eyes and mouths. Cotton embroidery floss or pearl cotton are easy to find and come in any color you might need. Use two or three ply of floss or a single strand of size 8 pearl cotton. Silk embroidery floss and novelty threads offer additional choices. Select a needle with an eye just large enough to thread the needle. A crewel needle or sharp, size 5 to 10, would be a good choice. A small embroidery hoop might be helpful but is not necessary. Project directions include a tracing pattern for embroidered details. The center of the patch (usually the face) is given to help you position the design. Fold the patch to find the center and place it over the tracing pattern, matching centers. Use a pencil to lightly mark the design. When beginning to embroider, leave a tail about ½" long on the back side and catch it with the stitches. When ending, run the threaded needle back through the embroidery on the wrong side. Trim tails carefully so they don't show through the flesh fabric.

**Stitches:** For features made with a single curved line, use outline stitch. For Jesus' mouth, use satin stitch. For eyelashes on Mary and the Heavenly Angel, use buttonhole stitch. See the project directions for how-to illustrations of these stitches.

**Adding Flat Trims:** Ribbon, lace and braid are all good choices for embellishing these quilts. Project directions will explain where trims go and when to add them. In general, you want to appliqué the trim to the fabric patch before piecing the patches so the ends will be caught in seams. Use thread to match the trim, not the background. Trims also can be machine appliquéd with invisible nylon sewing thread. Ribbon should be sewn on both edges, not down the middle, so it doesn't curl up.

## Embellishments Added After Quilting

Embellishments that are added after quilting are usually sewn through all layers of the quilt, working from the back side. Select thread to match the embellishment, except for buttons if you want a contrasting thread. If you choose embellishments that cannot be sewn and want to glue them instead, practice using extra embellishments, a glue gun or liquid glue and scrap fabric before using this technique on your quilt. Gluing cannot be undone.

**Pompoms:** These can be purchased ready-made, or you can make them yourself from yarn. Instructions are given on page 19.

**Buttons:** Select buttons that have holes through the button itself or choose buttons with a short shank. Avoid using buttons with holes through them for noses.

**Bells, Jewels, Ribbon Bows, Medallion Appliqués and Other Doodads:** These are sewn in place according to their type and location. For example, the bell on Tinker the Elf's hat is sewn just to the tip of his 3-D pieced hat, but the bells on his shoes are sewn through all layers of the quilt. The medallion appliqué on King III can be sewn through just the quilt top or through all layers as you wish.

# Santa Claus

**a right jolly old elf**

## Cutting Requirements

**Finished size:** 11¼" x 26¼"

| Ydg. | Fabric | Use | Cut |
|------|--------|-----|-----|
| ⅛ yd. | Dark Green Print | borders, tabs | 2 N, 2 F, 4 P |
| ¼ yd. | Red Print | binding, border corners | 1½" x 83", 4 A |
| ⅛ yd. | Light Green Print | background | 1 ZZ, 1 ZZr, 4 D, 2 LL |
| ¼ yd. | Red Print | Santa's hat, sleeves, pants | 1 WW, 2 D, 2 I |
| ¼ yd. | Red Print | Santa's coat | 1 W, 1 PP |
| ⅛ yd. | White-on-White | trim on hat and boots | 1 P, 2 I |
| | | pompom | 1 pompom (optional) |
| ⅛ yd. White Felt | | mustache, beard | 1 mustache, 2 D, 1 F |
| (or 1 square) | | | |
| ¼ yd. | Flesh Solid | face, hands | 1 W, 2 A |
| ⅛ yd. | Pink Solid | nose | 1 nose |
| ⅛ yd. | Black Satin | belt, boots | 2 A, 2 I, 2 C |
| ⅛ yd. | Gold Print | buttons, buckle | 2 buttons (optional), 1 A |
| ½ yd. | Light Solid | lining | 15" x 30" |

## Assembly

1. Lay out all patches as shown in the piecing diagram.

2. Sew hatband to hat as follows. As shown below, fold patch P in half horizontally and press. Position so that bottom edges of P and WW match; pin in place. Trim sides of P to match WW. Baste P in place, sewing ⅛" from edge.

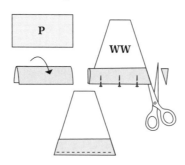

3. Join lettered patches as shown in the piecing diagram. For beard, trim seam allowances from the short ends of 2 felt D patches and one F patch.

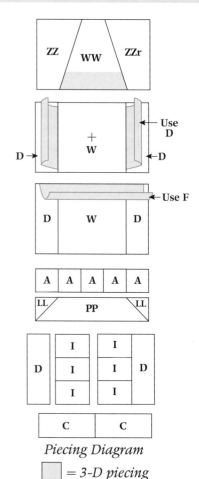

*Piecing Diagram*

☐ = 3-D piecing or appliqué

Catch sides of felt D patches in seams joining face (W) and background D patches. Catch felt F patch in seam joining face unit and body unit (patches D, W, D). Wherever possible, press seam allowances toward Santa and away from the background.

4 Carefully slash beard strip every ¼". The ends of the F piece can be curved as shown in the photo and the quilting diagram.

5 Referring to the general instructions, add border strips and corner squares. Press seam allowances toward the borders.

6 (optional) Appliqué mustache, pompom, nose, eyes and but-

tons (if they will not be made with a 3-D felt mustache and pompom and real buttons). If desired, put a small amount of polyester batting under the appliqués for puffiness.

7 Referring to the general instructions, assemble lining, batting and quilt top. Quilt in-the-ditch as shown in the quilting diagram. Add tabs and bind the quilt.

8 (optional) Add buttons for eyes and on coat; add pompom (if they were not appliquéd). Pin felt mustache to face and machine sew down through the middle.

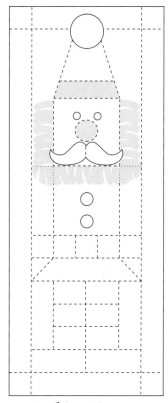

*Quilting Diagram*

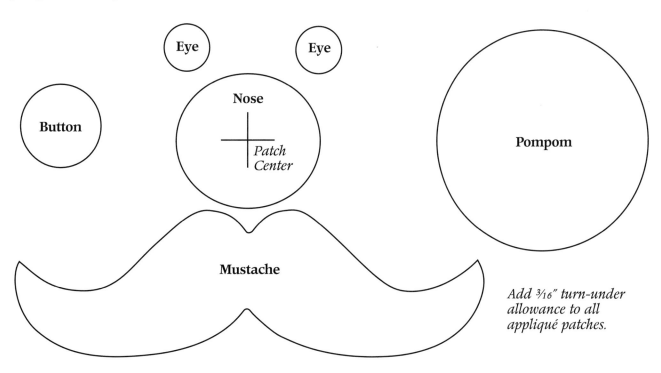

Eye

Eye

Button

Nose

Patch Center

Pompom

Mustache

*Add 3⁄16" turn-under allowance to all appliqué patches.*

# Mrs. Claus

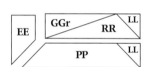

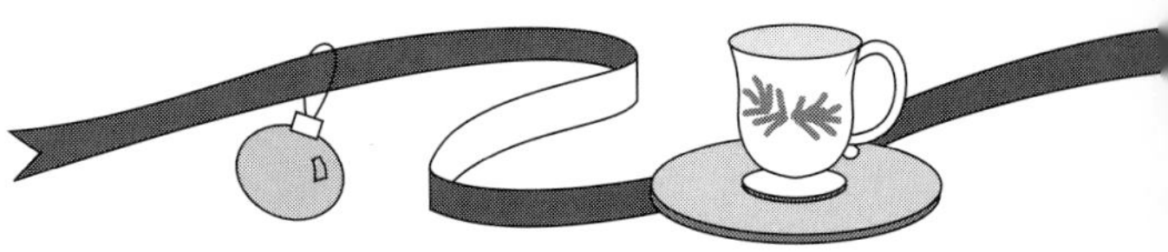

## the woman behind the man

## Cutting Requirements

**Finished size:** 11¼″ x 26¼″

| Ydg. | Fabric | Use | Cut |
|---|---|---|---|
| ⅛ yd. | Dark Green Print | borders, tabs | 2 N, 2 F, 4 P |
| ¼ yd. | Red Print | binding, border corners, nightgown | 1½″ x 83″, 4 A, 1 V, 1 GG, 1 GGr |
| ⅛ yd. | Light Green Print | background | 2 EE, 1 EEr, 1 GG, 2 GGr, 2 LL, 2 F |
| ⅛ yd. | Red Solid | Mrs. Claus's hat | 1 RR |
| ⅛ yd. | White-on-White | hat trim and pompom | 1 PP, 1 pompom |
| ⅛ yd. | Gray Print | hair | 1 EE, 1 EEr, 2 A |
| ¼ yd. | Flesh Solid | face, hands | 1 W, 2 A |
| ⅛ yd. | Pink Print | slippers, cheeks | 2 C, 2 cheeks |
| ½ yd. | Light Solid | lining | 15″ x 30″ |

**Also Needed:**
⅓ yd. ½″-wide white lace for trim on nightgown, 11¼″ white buttons, ¼ yd. gold cord & thread *or* gold floss for glasses, red floss for mouth, blue floss for eyes (optional), ¼ yd. narrow pink ribbon for bow

## Assembly

**1** Lay out all patches as shown in the piecing diagram.

**2** Sew hair over face as follows. As shown below, fold gray print patch A in half diagonally and press. Position A so that the square corners of triangle and the corner of flesh W match; pin in place. Repeat for other gray print A patch. Baste A triangles in place, sewing ⅛″ from edge.

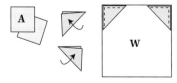

**3** Join lettered patches as shown in the piecing diagram. Note: Appliqué lace in place as shown in piecing diagram so that ends will be caught in seams. Wherever possible,

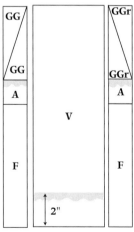

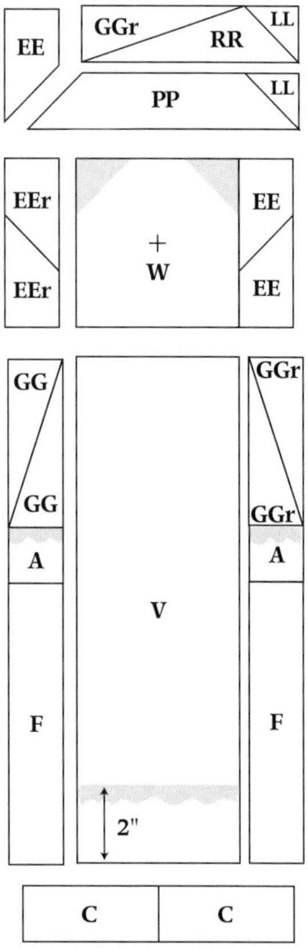

*Piecing Diagram*

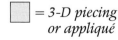
= 3-D piecing or appliqué

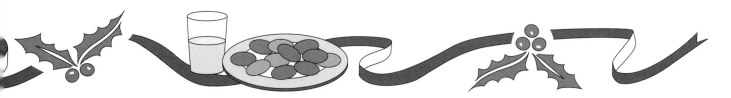

press seam allowances toward Mrs. Claus and away from the background.

4 Referring to the general instructions, add border strips and corner squares. Press seam allowances toward the borders.

5 (optional) Appliqué pompom. Embroider mouth and eyes. Embroider or couch glasses.

6 Referring to the general instructions, assemble lining, batting and quilt top. Quilt in-the-ditch as shown in the quilting diagram and quilt down the front of the night-gown. Add the tabs and bind the quilt.

7 (optional) Add buttons for eyes; add buttons on night-gown and pompom (if it was not appliquéd). Tie bow with ribbon and sew it at neck.

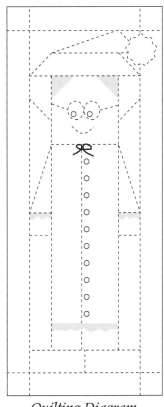

*Quilting Diagram*

*Outline Stitch*

## Couching

This technique allows you to lay cording on the quilt top and hold it in place with tiny stitches. Besides the cording, you will need thread to match the cording. Sulky gold metallic thread is excellent for couching gold cording such as we used on Mrs. Claus's glasses. The ends of the cording can either be buried in a seam or they can be gently pulled through the quilt top by threading them through a needle. Couching stitches are tiny, coming up directly under the cording and going back through the quilt top directly under the cording. Couching stitches usually won't show at all.

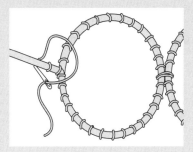

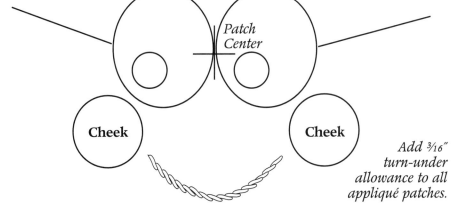

*Patch Center*

**Cheek**

**Cheek**

*Add 3/16" turn-under allowance to all appliqué patches.*

**Pompom**

# Frosty the Snowman

## a jolly, happy soul

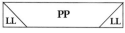

## Cutting Requirements

**Finished size:** 11¼" x 26¼"

| Ydg. | Fabric | Use | Cut |
|---|---|---|---|
| ⅛ yd. | Blue Print | borders, tabs | 2 N, 2 F, 4 P |
| ¼ yd. | Purple Print | binding, border corners, hat | 1½" x 83", 4 A, 1 W, 1 F |
| ⅛ yd. | Light Blue Print | background | 2 D, 1 AA, 1 AAr, 2 LL |
| ¼ yd. | White Print | snowman | 1 W, 1 R, 1 PP |
| ⅛ yd. | Green Print | hatband | 1 D |
| ⅛ yd. | Red Plaid | scarf | 1 PP, 1 X |
| ⅛ yd. | Red Solid | mittens | 1 mitten, 1 mitten reversed |
| ⅛ yd. | Red Print | flower on hat | 1 flower and 1 reversed (if 3-D appliquéd) or 1 flower (if appliquéd) |
| ⅛ yd. | Gold Print | pipe | 1 pipe bowl |
| ½ yd. | Light Solid | lining | 15" x 30" |

**Also Needed:**
3½" narrow black ribbon    pipe stem

## Creative Options

**Flower:** make a 3-D appliqué (see page 4) *or* appliqué patch

**Flower Center:** use a ¾" button *or* appliqué circle

**Hatband:** fabric *or* braid

**Eyes:** use ¾" buttons *or* appliqué circles

**Nose:** use a ⅝" button *or* appliqué circle

**Buttons:** use ⅞" buttons *or* appliqué circles

## Assembly

1  Lay out all patches as shown in the piecing diagram.

2  If you want to use fabric for the hatband, fold green print D patch in half lengthwise. As shown below, position folded strip along one edge of purple W, matching raw edges. Baste hatband in place, sewing ⅛"

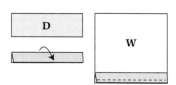

from edge of patch. If you want to use braid instead, appliqué it in place ¼" from one edge of W before joining patches.

3  Join lettered patches as shown in the piecing diagram. Note: To prepare the hanging part of the scarf, fold red plaid X in

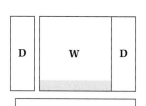

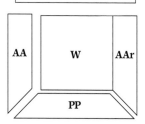

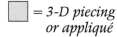

*Piecing Diagram*

☐ = 3-D piecing or appliqué

half with right sides together; sew. Turn this tube right side out and press flat. As shown here, catch one end of tube in the seam joining the scarf and

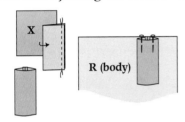

the snowman's body (R). Wherever possible, press seam allowances toward the hat, scarf and snowman. If necessary, trim dark seam allowances to prevent them showing through the white fabric.

4 Appliqué mittens, centering them on sides of the snowman's R patch. If desired, cut mittens from batting (about ¼" smaller all around) and place under appliqués before sewing. Appliqué flower and flower

center on hat if they will not be done in 3-D appliqué.

5 Referring to the general instructions, add border strips and corner squares. Press seam allowances toward borders.

6 Appliqué eyes, nose and buttons if they will not be done with buttons. Appliqué black ribbon pipe stem and gold print pipe bowl. Pipe bowl will overlap the border.

7 Referring to the general instructions, assemble lining, batting and quilt top. Quilt in-the-ditch as shown in the quilting diagram. Add tabs and bind the quilt.

8 Add 3-D flower and buttons for eyes, nose and on snowman if they were not appliquéd. Clip ¾" into lower edge of scarf at ⅛" intervals.

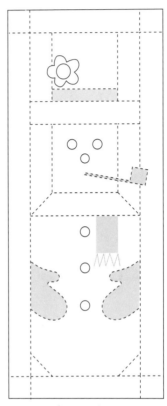

*Quilting Diagram*

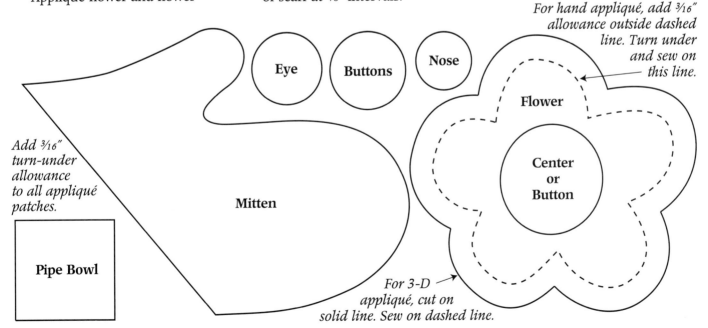

*For hand appliqué, add ³⁄₁₆" allowance outside dashed line. Turn under and sew on this line.*

*Add ³⁄₁₆" turn-under allowance to all appliqué patches.*

Eye

Buttons

Nose

Flower

Center or Button

Mitten

Pipe Bowl

*For 3-D appliqué, cut on solid line. Sew on dashed line.*

# Rudy the Reindeer

## with his nose so bright

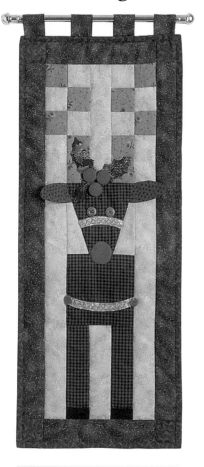

## Cutting Requirements

**Finished size:** 11¼" x 26¼"

| Ydg. | Fabric | Use | Cut |
|---|---|---|---|
| ⅛ yd. | Blue Print | borders, tabs | 2 N, 2 F, 4 P |
| ¼ yd. | Purple Print | binding, border corners | 1½" x 83", 4 A |
| ⅛ yd. | Light Blue Print | background | 6 A, 1 F, 2 J, 1 GG, 1 GGr, 1 E |
| ⅛ yd. | Light Brown Print | antlers | 6 A, 2 B |
| ¼ yd. | Brown Plaid | reindeer face and body | 1 WW, 1 W, 2 E |
| ⅛ yd. | Black Solid | hooves | 2 A |
| ⅛ yd. | Rust Print | ears | 2 ears and 2 ears reversed |
| ⅛ yd. | Green Print | holly | 1 of each holly leaf |
| ⅛ yd. | Red Solid | nose | 1 nose |
| ½ yd. | Light Solid | lining | 15" x 30" |
| **Also Needed:** | | | |
| ¼ yd. | gold braid | harness and bridle | |

## Creative Options

**Holly Berries:** use ¾" covered buttons *or* appliqué circles

**Eyes:** use ⅝" buttons *or* appliqué circles

**Harness:** use ⅝" buttons *or* appliqué circles

## Assembly

**1** Lay out all patches as shown in the piecing diagram.

**2** Add hooves as follows. Fold black A patch in half. As shown below, position folded A on right side of brown plaid E, matching raw edges. Repeat for other hoof. Baste hooves in place, sewing ⅛" from edge.

**3** Join lettered patches as shown in the piecing diagram. Note: Sew gold braid to face (WW) and body (W). The ends of the gold braid will be caught in seams as the quilt top is pieced. For the ears, sew 1 ear and 1 ear reversed with right sides together along curved edge. Clip curves. Turn ear right side out; press. Repeat for other ear. Catch ears in

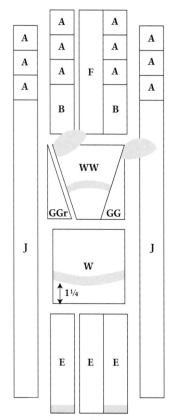

*Piecing Diagram*

☐ = 3-D piecing or appliqué

seams when sewing the face (WW) patch to GG and GGr, positioning ears ¼" from top of WW. Wherever possible, press seam allowances toward the reindeer.

**4** Appliqué holly. Appliqué harness "buttons," holly berries, eyes and nose if they will not be made with buttons.

**5** Referring to the general instructions, add border strips and corner squares. Press seam allowances toward the borders.

**6** Referring to the general instructions, assemble lining, batting and quilt top. Quilt in-the-ditch and on holly as shown in the quilting diagram. Add tabs and bind the quilt.

**7** Add buttons for harness, holly berries, eyes and nose if they were not appliquéd.

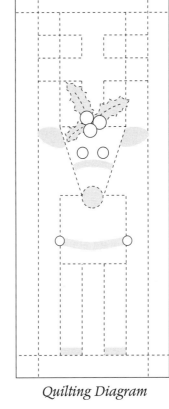

*Quilting Diagram*

*Add ³⁄₁₆" turn-under allowance to all appliqué patches.*

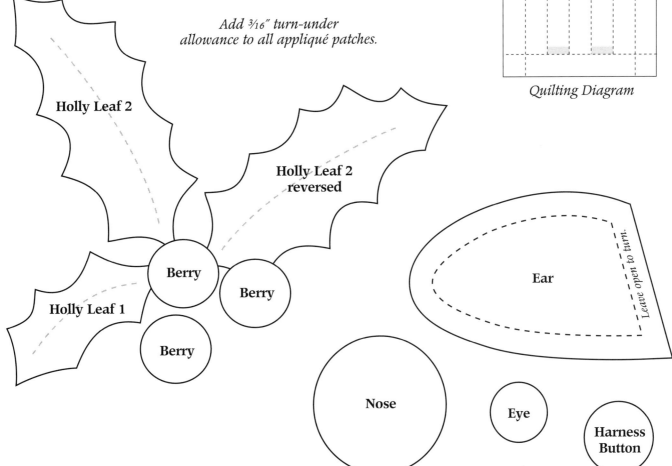

# The Nutcracker

**a suite
Christmas tradition**

## Cutting Requirements

**Finished size:** 11¼" x 26¼"

| Ydg. | Fabric | Use | Cut |
|------|--------|-----|-----|
| ⅛ yd. | Green Print | borders, tabs | 2 N, 2 F, 4 P |
| ¼ yd. | Red Print | binding, border corners | 1½" x 83", 4 A |
| ⅛ yd. | Light Blue Print | background | 1 GG, 1 GGr, 2 D, 2 E |
| ¼ yd. | Flesh | face and hands | 1 W, 2 A |
| ⅛ yd. | Brown Print | mustache | 1 mustache |
| ⅛ yd. | Blue Print | hat, trousers | 1 VV, 2 Q |
| ⅛ yd. | Red Print | jacket | 4 D |
| ⅛ yd. | Black Satin | brim of hat, belt, shoes | 2 hat brims, 2 A, 2 C |
| ½ yd. | Light Solid | lining | 15" x 30" |
| **Also Needed:** | | | |
| ⅛ yd. ½"-wide gold braid | | trim on cuffs | |
| ⅛ yd. gold fringe (optional) | | epaulets | |

## Creative Options

**Eyes:** use ½" buttons *or* appliqué circles

**Hat Buttons:** use 1" buttons *or* appliqué circles

**Mustache:** appliqué patch *or* make a 3-D mustache

**Epaulets:** use gold fringe and trim to 1" long *or* appliqué patches

## Assembly

**1** Lay out all patches as shown in the piecing diagram.

**2** Sew hat brim over face as follows. Place 2 black hat brims right sides together and sew curved edge. Turn brim right side out and press flat. As shown below, position and pin brim on flesh W. Baste brim in place, sewing ⅛" from edge.

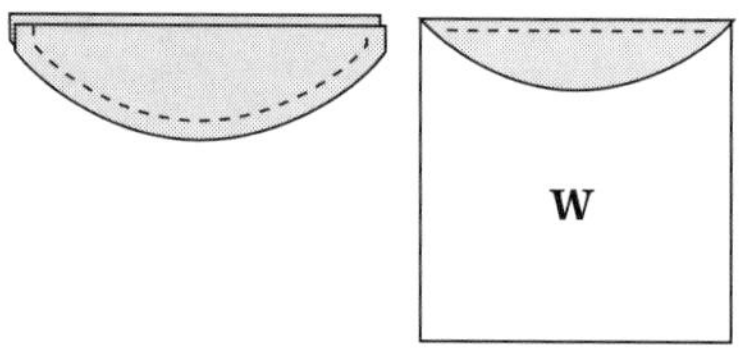

**3** For trim on sleeves, appliqué gold braid ¾" from end of red print D patch. Repeat for another red print D patch. Appliqué epaulet to top of each sleeve or baste gold fringe in place. (Gold fringe can also be added later if you prefer.)

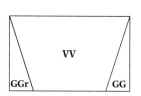

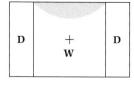

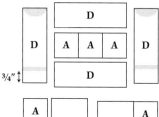

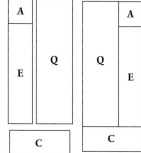

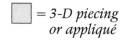

*Piecing Diagram*

☐ = 3-D piecing or appliqué

4 Join lettered patches as shown in the piecing diagram. Wherever possible, press seam allowances toward the nut-cracker.

5 Appliqué mustache. Appliqué eyes and hat buttons if they will not be made with real buttons. If desired, put a small amount of batting underneath appliqués for puffiness.

6 Referring to the general instructions, add border strips and corner squares. Press seam allowances toward the borders.

7 Referring to the general instructions, assemble lining, batting and quilt top. Quilt in-the-ditch as shown in the quilting diagram. Add tabs and bind the quilt.

8 Add buttons for eyes and on the hat if they were not appliquéd. Sew gold fringe for epaulets if it was not added earlier, and trim so it is about 1″ long.

*Quilting Diagram*

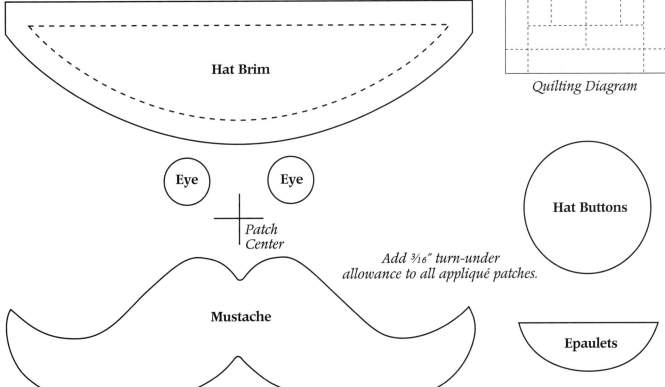

**Hat Brim**

**Eye**      **Eye**

Patch Center

*Add ³⁄₁₆″ turn-under allowance to all appliqué patches.*

**Hat Buttons**

**Mustache**

**Epaulets**

# Sugar Plum Fairy

**dances on her toes**

## Cutting Requirements

**Finished size:** 11¼" x 26¼"

| Ydg. | Fabric | Use | Cut |
|---|---|---|---|
| ⅛ yd. | Green Print | borders, tabs | 2 N, 2 F, 4 P |
| ¼ yd. | Red Print | binding, border corners | 1½" x 83", 4 A |
| ⅛ yd. | Light Blue Print | background | 6 LL, 2 D, 1 E, 1 DDr, 2 A, 1 P, 1 F |
| ¼ yd. | Flesh | face and body | 1 MM, 2 EEr, 1 E, 1 OO, 1 II, 1 AA, 1 B, 1 A, 1 JJr |
| ⅛ yd. | Brown Print | hair | 1 JJ, 1 JJr, 1 A, 1 C |
| ⅛ yd. | Pink Check | top of tutu | 1 P |
| ⅛ yd. | Pink Print | skirt of tutu | 1 D, 1 LL, 1 F |
| ⅛ yd. | Pink Satin | ballet slippers | 1 A, 1 EE |
| ½ yd. | Light Solid | lining | 15" x 30" |

**Also Needed:**

| | | |
|---|---|---|
| Red floss | | mouth |
| 1½ yds. ¼"-wide pink ribbon | | straps on tutu, ties on ballet slippers, bow in hair |

## Creative Options

**Ballet Slippers:** use satin *or* cotton fabric

**Shoe Straps:** use ¼" satin ribbon and add a couple of bows *or* appliqué bias strips

## Assembly

**1** Lay out all patches as shown in the piecing diagram.

**2** Sew hair over face as follows. Fold brown print C patch in half lengthwise. As shown below, position and pin folded C strip on flesh MM. Trim C to match shape of MM. Baste hair in place, sewing ⅛" from edge.

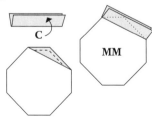

**3** Appliqué ribbon to shoulders and legs as shown here.

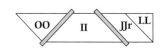

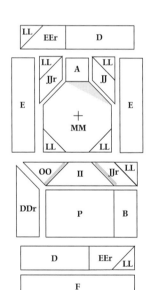

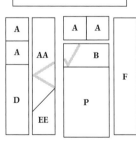

*Piecing Diagram*

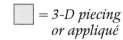 = 3-D piecing or appliqué

16

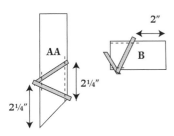

**4** Join lettered patches as shown in the piecing diagram. Wherever possible, press seam allowances toward the ballerina.

*Quilting Diagram*

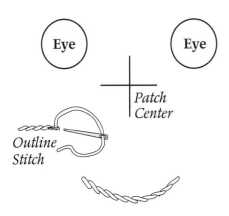

**5** Appliqué eyes if they will not be made with buttons. Embroider mouth.

**6** Referring to the general instructions, add border strips and corner squares. Press seam allowances toward borders.

**7** Referring to the general instructions, assemble lining,

batting and quilt top. Quilt in-the-ditch as shown in the quilting diagram. Add tabs and bind the quilt.

**8** Add buttons for eyes if they were not appliquéd. Cut remaining ribbon in 3 pieces; tie each piece in a bow. Sew bows in place on forehead and legs.

## Nutcracker Suite

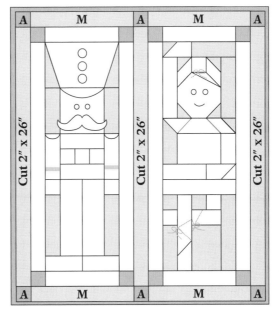

The Nutcracker and the Sugar Plum Fairy can be combined to make a quilt that finishes 26¼" x 29¼".

**1.** Make the two quilt tops as explained in project directions.

**2.** Cut 3 strips 2" x 26" and 4 M strips. Cut 6 A patches. Cut binding 1½" x 120". Cut lining 30" x 33". Cut batting 30" x 33".

**3.** Join the quilt tops alternately

with the long strips. Press seam allowances toward the strips. Join 3 A squares alternately with 2 M strips to make top border. Repeat to make bottom border. Press seam allowances toward the M strips. Sew borders to top and bottom of quilt.

**4.** Assemble lining, batting and quilt top as explained in the general instructions. Quilt, add tabs (if desired) and bind.

# Pixie the Elf

## takes charge of the lollipops

## Cutting Requirements

**Finished size:** 11 1/4" x 26 1/4"

| Ydg. | Fabric | Use | Cut |
|---|---|---|---|
| 1/8 yd. | Green Print | borders, tabs | 2 N, 2 F, 4 P |
| 1/4 yd. | Red Print | binding, border corners, hat, sleeves, skirt | 1 1/2" x 83", 4 A, 1 WW, 1 T, 1 Tr, 1 B, 1 EE, 1 PP |
| 1/8 yd. | White/Red Print | background | 1 NN, 1 NNr, 3 OO, 1 T, 1 Tr, 1 EE, 1 DD, 1 DDr, 1 E |
| 1/4 yd. | Flesh | face, ears, hands | 1 MM, 1 S, 1 Sr, 2 A |
| 1/8 yd. | Light Brown Print | hair | 2 LL, 2 OO |
| 1/8 yd. | Green Print | dress, shoes | 1 P, 1 A, 3 B, 2 LL |
| 1/8 yd. | Red/White Stripe | leggings, lollipop | 2 D, 1 lollipop |
| 1/8 yd. | Gold Print | lollipop stick | 1 lollipop stick |
| 1/2 yd. | Light Solid | lining | 15" x 30" |
| **Also Needed:** | | | |
| Red floss | | mouth | |
| 1/2 yd. narrow red ribbon | | hair ties | |

## Assembly

1 Lay out all patches as shown in the piecing diagram.

2 Join lettered patches as shown in the piecing diagram. Appliqué lollipop patches in place as shown in piecing diagram so that ends will be caught in seams. If necessary, appliqué the lollipop after the piecing is finished, then open seams and tuck in ends before closing seams. Wherever possible, press seam allowances toward the elf and away from the background.

3 Referring to the general instructions, add border strips and corner squares. Press seam allowances toward the borders.

4 (optional) Appliqué hat pompom. Appliqué eyes, nose and

*Piecing Diagram*

▢ = *3-D piecing or appliqué*

## Creative Options

**Pompom:** make a pompom from yarn *or* appliqué circle
**Hat Buttons:** use real 3/4" buttons *or* appliqué circle patches
**Eyes:** use 5/8" buttons *or* appliqué circles
**Shoes:** use 3/4" jingle bells *or* purchased yarn pompoms

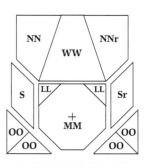

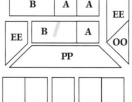

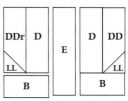

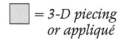

hat buttons if they will not be done with real buttons. Embroider mouth.

5 Referring to the general instructions, assemble lining, batting and quilt top. Quilt in-the-ditch around patches as shown in the quilting diagram. Add tabs and bind the quilt.

6 Cut ribbon into 2 pieces; tie each piece in a bow. Sew bows in place on hair. Sew bells or add pompoms on points of shoes. Add yarn pompom and buttons for eyes, nose and hat if they were not appliquéd.

*Quilting Diagram*

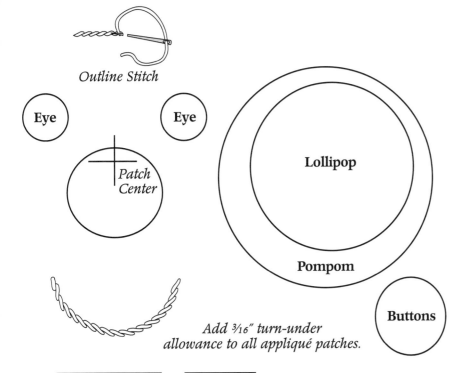

*Outline Stitch*

**Eye**   **Eye**

*Patch Center*

**Lollipop**

**Pompom**

**Buttons**

*Add 3/16" turn-under allowance to all appliqué patches.*

**Lollipop Stick**

## Making a Pompom

Three of the quilts in this book include pompoms: Santa Claus, Mrs. Claus and Pixie the Elf. Follow these steps if you want to make a pompom using worsted-weight knitting yarn.

**1.** Use a 2"-wide ruler. Tape a double strand of yarn to one side.

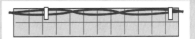

**2.** Wrap yarn closely over a 3" width and allow the yarn to build up to a depth of at least ½".

**3.** Untape the yarn and tie it tightly around the wrapped yarn. (This is easier to do with two people.) Make two or three square knots so the tie is very tight and secure.

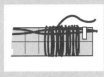

**4.** Slide the yarn off ruler.

**5.** Cut thread loops. Holding onto the yarn ties, fluff pompom and trim ends to make a circle in the desired size. (Trimming is like pruning a hedge.)

**6.** Hand sew pompom in place, catching the tied knot with the stitches.

# Tinker the Elf

## a busy little helper

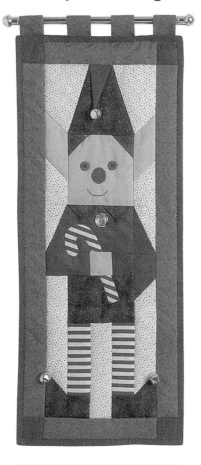

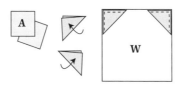

## Cutting Requirements

**Finished size:** 11¼" x 26¼"

| Ydg. | Fabric | Use | Cut |
|---|---|---|---|
| ⅛ yd. | Green Print | borders, tabs | 2 N, 2 F, 4 P |
| ¼ yd. | Red Print | binding, border corners, shirt, hat point | 1½" x 83", 5 A, 1 T, 1 Tr, 1 P, 1 B, 1 EE, 1 hat point and 1 hat point reversed (for 3-D piecing) |
| ⅛ yd. | White/Red Print | background | 1 NN, 1 NNr, 1 EE, 1 EEr, 1 T, 1 Tr, 1 Zr, 1 E, 1 LL, 1 AA |
| ¼ yd. | Flesh | face, ears, hand | 1 W, 1 S, 1 Sr, 1 A |
| ⅛ yd. | Light Brown Print | hair | 2 A |
| ⅛ yd. | Green Print | hat, collar, shorts, shoes | 1 WW, 4 collar points, 1 P, 2 A, 1 EE, 1EEr |
| ⅛ yd. | Red/White Stripe | leggings, candy cane | 2 D, 1 candy cane |
| ½ yd. | Light Solid | lining | 15" x 30" |

**Also Needed:**

| | | |
|---|---|---|
| Red floss | | mouth |

## Assembly

**1** Lay out all patches as shown in the piecing diagram.

**2** Sew hair over face as follows. As shown below, fold brown print patch A in half diagonally and press. Position A so that the square corners of triangle and the corner of flesh W match; pin in place. Repeat for other brown print A patch. Baste A triangles in place, sewing ⅛" from edge.

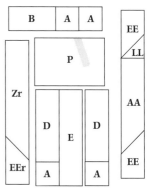

**3** Add collar as follows. Placing right sides together, sew 2 collar points along short sides. Trim point. Turn right side out and press. Repeat for other collar point. Position collar

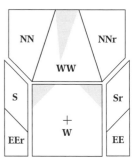

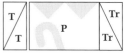

*Piecing Diagram*

▢ = 3-D piecing or appliqué

## Creative Options

**Hat Point:** use 3-D piecing *or* appliqué patch

**Pompom:** use a jingle bell *or* a purchased yarn pompom

**Eyes:** use ⅝" buttons *or* appliqué circles

**Shirt Button:** use a real ⅞" button *or* appliqué circle

**Hat and Shoes:** use ¾" jingle bells *or* purchased yarn pompoms

points on right side of red print P. Baste collar points in place.

**4** Join lettered patches as shown in the piecing diagram. Appliqué the candy cane after the piecing is finished, then open seams and tuck in ends before closing seams. Wherever possible, press seam allowances toward elf and away from the background.

**5** (optional) Make and add 3-D pieced hat point. Appliqué eyes and shirt button if they will not be done with real

buttons. Appliqué nose. Embroider mouth.

**6** Referring to the general instructions, add border strips and corner squares. Press seam allowances toward the borders.

**7** Referring to the general instructions, assemble lining, batting and quilt top. Quilt in-the-ditch as shown in quilting diagram and quilt center of Tinker's shorts. Add the tabs and bind the quilt.

**8** Sew bells or add pompoms on point of hat and points of shoes. Add buttons for eyes, nose and shirt button if they were not appliquéd.

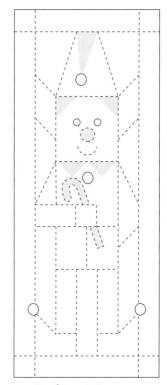

*Quilting Diagram*

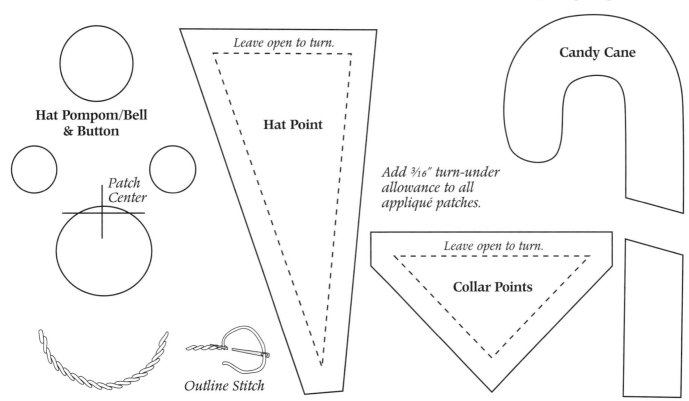

*Leave open to turn.*

**Hat Pompom/Bell & Button**

*Patch Center*

*Outline Stitch*

**Hat Point**

**Candy Cane**

*Add ³⁄₁₆" turn-under allowance to all appliqué patches.*

*Leave open to turn.*

**Collar Points**

# Christmas Trees

## to decorate
## any way you want

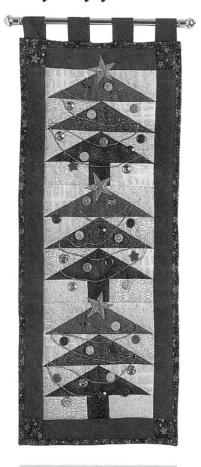

## Cutting Requirements

**Finished size:** 11¼" x 26¼"

| Ydg. | Fabric | Use | Cut |
|---|---|---|---|
| ⅛ yd. | Red Print | borders, tabs, | 2 N, 2 F, 4 P |
| ¼ yd. | Navy Print | binding, border corners | 1½" x 83", 4 A |
| ¼ yd. | various Yellow Prints | background | 9 U, 9 Ur, 6 B |
| ⅛ yd. | various Green Prints | trees | 9 QQ |
| ⅛ yd. | Brown Print | tree trunks | 3 A |
| ⅛ yd. | Gold Print | stars | 3 stars (if appliquéd) |
| ½ yd. | Light Solid | lining | 15" x 30" |

**Also Needed:**
4 yds. gold cord and gold thread

## Assembly

**1** Lay out all patches as shown in the piecing diagram.

**2** Join lettered patches as shown in the piecing diagram. Press seam allowances at the upper edges of QQ patches toward the background; press other seam allowances toward the trees.

**3** Referring to the general instructions, add border strips and corner squares. Press seam allowances toward the borders.

**4** (optional) Appliqué circle ornaments. If desired, put a small amount of polyester batting under appliqués for puffiness. Appliqué star patches or purchased stars.

**5** Referring to the general instructions, assemble lining, batting and quilt top. Quilt in-

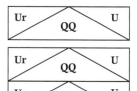

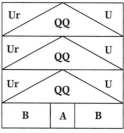

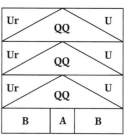

*Piecing Diagram*

the-ditch as shown in the quilting diagram. Add tabs and bind the quilt.

**6** Referring to directions at right, couch the gold cording to make garland swags on the tree. You can either tack the cording just at the ends to let it hang free, or you can couch it more closely to hold it firmly on the quilt.

**7** (optional) Sew buttons, sequins and small objects to decorate the trees.

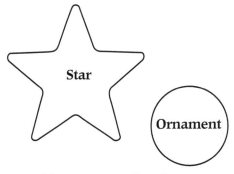

**Star**

**Ornament**

*Add ³⁄₁₆" turn-under allowance to all appliqué patches.*

The Christmas Trees quilt can be decorated as creatively as you would trim a real tree. Any item that is about ½" to 1" will work. Besides buttons and gold cording as you can see in the photograph, you might want to consider adding:

❊ charms
❊ mini ornaments
❊ ribbon for garland
❊ ribbon roses
❊ tiny photographs
❊ miniatures
❊ beads

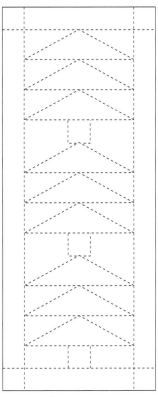

*Quilting Diagram*

## Garland

The garland we used on our Christmas Trees quilt is called bead yarn, but any kind of gold cording will work fine. We used a single strand of Sulky metallic gold thread to "couch" the garland and hold it in place on top of the quilt.

To do couching, simply lay the cording where you want it and hand sew with one or two stitches to hold the cording in place.

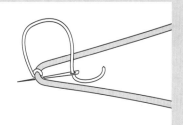

The couching stitches can be spaced as closely together or as far apart as you wish. Our garland is couched at intervals of about 2". The ends of the cording can be caught in the seams by threading a tapestry needle and gently guiding it through the seam between the threads.

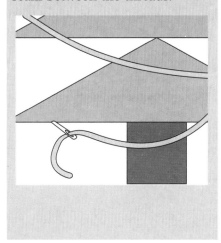

# Starry Night

**the stars shone brightly that long-ago night**

## Creative Options

**Flower Stars:** make 3-D appliqués (see page 4) *or* appliqué patches

**Buttons:** use real ¾" buttons or appliqué circle patches

## Cutting Requirements

**Finished size:** 11¼" x 26¼"

| Ydg. | Fabric | Use | Cut |
|---|---|---|---|
| ⅛ yd. | Red Print | borders, tabs | 2 N, 2 F, 4 P |
| ¼ yd. | Navy Print | binding, border corners | 1½" x 83", 4 A |
| ⅛ yd. | Blue Print | background | 2 X, 2 YY, 2 DD, 2 DDr, 2 HH |
| ⅛ yd. | Purple Print | background | 1 YYr, 1 X, 1 DD, 1 DDr, 1 HHr |
| ⅛ yd. | various Yellow Prints | stars | 3 T, 3 Tr, 9 LL, 3 P, 5 flower stars and 5 reversed (if 3-D appliquéd) *or* 5 flower stars (if appliquéd) |
| ½ yd. | Light Solid | lining | 15" x 30" |

## Assembly

**1** Lay out all patches as shown in the piecing diagram.

**2** Join lettered patches as shown in the piecing diagram. Wherever possible, press seam allowances toward the background.

**3** Referring to the general instructions, add border strips and corner squares. Press seam allowances toward the borders.

**4** (optional) Appliqué flower stars and circle centers. If desired, put a small amount of polyester batting under appliqués for puffiness.

**5** Referring to the general instructions, assemble lining, batting and quilt top. Quilt in-the-ditch as shown in the quilting diagram. Add tabs and bind the quilt.

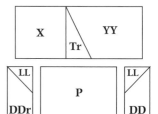

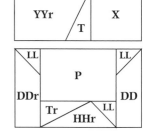

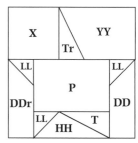

*Piecing Diagram*

24

**6** (optional) Make and add 3-D flower stars if they were not appliquéd. Sew buttons in place for centers of flower stars.

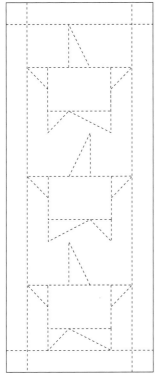

*Quilting Diagram*

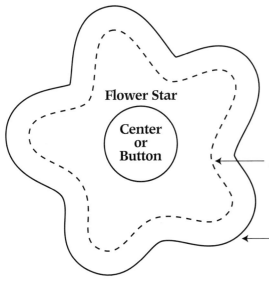

**Flower Star**

**Center or Button**

For hand appliqué, add ³⁄₁₆″ allowance outside dashed line. Turn under and sew on this line.

For 3-D appliqué, cut on solid line. Sew on dashed line.

## *Signs of the Season*

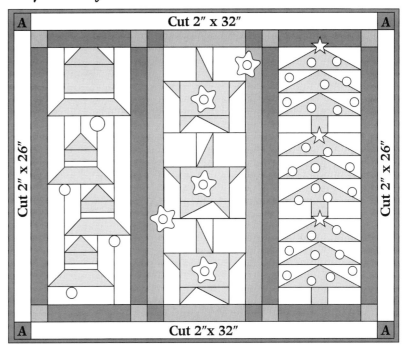

Joyful Bells, Starry Night and Christmas Trees can be combined to make a quilt that finishes 35¼″ x 29¼″.

**1.** Make the three quilt tops as explained in project directions. Join them side by side with the Starry Night quilt top in the middle.

**2.** Cut 2 borders 2″ x 32″ and 2 borders 2″ x 26″. Cut 4 A patches for corner squares. Cut binding 1½″ x 137″. Cut lining 39″ x 33″. Cut batting 39″ x 33″.

**3.** Sew short borders to sides of quilt top. Sew A squares to ends of long borders. Sew long borders to top and bottom of quilt.

**4.** Assemble lining, batting and quilt top as explained in the general instructions. Quilt, add tabs (if desired) and bind. Embellish the quilt as you wish.

# Joyful Bells

## ring in the holidays

**Bell Trim:** use fabric for
3-D piecing *or* use gold
braid

**Clappers:** use one 1¼"
and 3 1" buttons *or*
appliqué circles

## Cutting Requirements

**Finished size: 11¼" x 26¼"**

| Ydg. | Fabric | Use | Cut |
|---|---|---|---|
| ⅛ yd. | Red Print | borders, tabs, bell clappers (optional) | 2 N, 2 F, 4 P<br>1 large circle, 3 small circles |
| ¼ yd. | Navy Print | binding, border corners | 1½" x 83", 4 A |
| ¼ yd. | various Yellow Prints | background | 2 AA, 2 AAr, 6 LL, 1 EE, 1 EEr, 1 FFr, 1 DD, 1 DDr, 1 Y, 2 E |
| ⅛ yd. | Dk. Blue Print | bells | 1 P, 3 B |
| ⅛ yd. | Med Blue Print | bells | 1 II, 1 PP, 3 OO, 3 TT |
| ⅛ yd. | Gold Print | trim on bells (optional) | 1 D, 3 B |
| ½ yd. | Light Solid | lining | 15" x 30" |

## Assembly

**1** Lay out all patches as shown in the piecing diagram.

**2** If you want to use fabric trimming on the bells, first trim off ½" along one long edge of each gold B and D strip. Fold strips in half lengthwise. As shown below, position one folded strip over one long edge of each blue B and P patch, matching raw edges. Baste trimming in place, sewing ⅛" from edge of patch. If you want to use braid trimming, appliqué it in place after sewing blue rectangles to PP and TT bell pieces and before adding background patches so that ends of braid will be caught in seams.

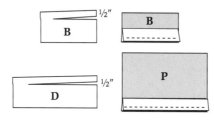

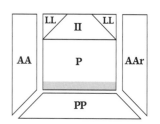

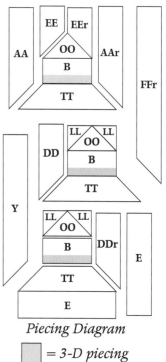

*Piecing Diagram*

☐ = *3-D piecing or appliqué*

**3** Join lettered patches as shown in the piecing diagram, working from the bottom up. Note: Find information about setting in patches on this page. Wherever possible, press seam allowances toward the bells.

**4** Referring to the general instructions, add border strips and corner squares. Press seam allowances toward borders.

**5** (optional) Appliqué circle clappers. If desired, put a small amount of polyester batting under appliqués for puffiness.

**6** Referring to the general instructions, assemble lining, batting and quilt top. Quilt in-the-ditch as shown in the quilting diagram. Add tabs and bind the quilt.

**7** (optional) Sew buttons in place for clappers.

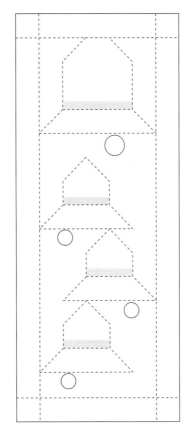
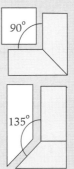
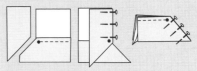

*Quilting Diagram*

( **Small Bell Clapper** )   ( **Large Bell Clapper** )

*Add ³⁄₁₆″ turn-under allowance to all appliqué patches.*

## Set-In Patches

Several of the quilts in this book include angled patches that must be set in. Patch DD is an example of an angled patch that will be set into the angle created by the bell shape.

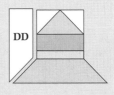

To sew a set-in patch, first join the patches that make the widest possible angle. As a general rule, avoid setting patches in angles less than 90°. The wider the angle, the easier it is to sew.

The most important thing to remember about sewing a set-in patch is that you sew only on the seam lines, not to the edge of the patch. Sew one side of the patch. Stop and reposition, then sew the remaining side.

You may find it helpful to place the patch you are setting in on the under side. That way, you will be able to see where the line of stitching should begin.

# Heavenly Angel

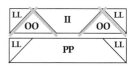

## hark the herald angel sings

### Creative Options

**Halo:** use cotton fabric *or* gold lamé fabric
**Wings:** appliqué narrow gold ribbon along seams of wings

## Cutting Requirements

**Finished size:** 11¼" x 26¼"

| Ydg. | Fabric | Use | Cut |
|---|---|---|---|
| ⅛ yd. | Green Print | borders, tabs | 2 N, 2 F, 4 P |
| ¼ yd. | Gold Print | binding, border corners | 1½" x 83", 4 A |
| ⅛ yd. | Dark Blue Print | background | 2 LL, 1 II, 1 DD, 1 DDr |
| ¼ yd. | Flesh | face and hands | 1 MM, 2 LL |
| ⅛ yd. | Brown Print | hair | 2 LL, 1 JJ, 1 JJr, 2 OO |
| ⅛ yd. | Yellow Print | halo | 1 PP, 1 DD, 1 DDr, 2 LL |
| ⅛ yd. | White Print #1 | wings | 2 OO, 2 II, 1 S, 1 Sr |
| ⅛ yd. | White Print #2 | wings | 2 LL, 2 S, 2 Sr |
| ⅛ yd. | Pink Print | robe | 1 Y, 1 Yr |
| ⅛ yd. | Dark Pink Print | robe top and center | 1 II, 1 K |
| ⅛ yd. | Maroon Print | robe bottom | 1 AA, 1 AAr |
| ⅛ yd. | Pink Solid | mouth | 1 mouth |
| ½ yd. | Light Solid | lining | 15" x 30" |

**Also Needed:**

| | | |
|---|---|---|
| Blue floss | eyes | |
| 1 yd. narrow gold ribbon | trim on wings | |

## Assembly

**1** Lay out all patches as shown in the piecing diagram.

**2** To make 3-D hair bangs, place brown LL patches right sides together and sew along two short sides. Trim corner and turn right side out. Pin in place on MM and baste ⅛" from edges of patches. With right sides together, sew brown print JJ and JJr along two sides as shown below. Trim corner and turn right side out. Position this piece on MM. Pin and baste.

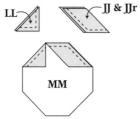

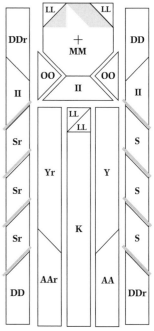

*Piecing Diagram*

☐ = 3-D piecing or appliqué

*continued on page 33*

28

*Santa Claus,*
*Mrs. Claus*

*The Nutcracker and*
*Sugar Plum Fairy*

*Heavenly Angel,
Shepherd*

*Joyful Bells,
Starry Night,
Christmas
Trees*

*Mary & Baby Jesus, Joseph*

*King I, King II, King III*

*Frosty the Snowman,*
*Rudy the Reindeer*

*Pixie the Elf,*
*Tinker the Elf*

**3** Join lettered patches as shown in the piecing diagram. (See the box on this page for more information about adding the gold ribbon as the piecing progresses.) Wherever possible, press seam allowances toward the angel. If dark seam allowances show through light fabric, trim seam allowances.

**4** Appliqué the mouth. Embroider the eyes with buttonhole stitch using two strands of blue floss.

*Patch Center*

Add ³⁄₁₆" turn-under allowance to appliqué patch.

**Mouth**

*Buttonhole Stitch*

**5** Referring to the general instructions, add border strips and corner squares. Press seam allowances toward borders.

**6** Referring to the general instructions, assemble lining, batting and quilt top. Quilt in-the-ditch as shown in the quilting diagram. Add the tabs and bind the quilt.

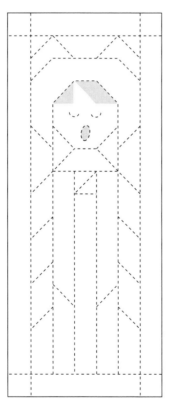

*Quilting Diagram*

## Using Gold Ribbon and Fabric

The gold ribbon should be appliquéd over seam lines as the piecing progresses so that ends can be caught in seams. Cut ribbon into 12 pieces 3" long. Appliqué can be done with a narrow machine zigzag stitch using gold or invisible thread, or it can be done with hand-sewn blind stitching. Refer to the piecing diagram. For the lower parts of the angel's wings, appliqué the gold ribbon after assembling the side columns of patches. For the upper parts of the wings, appliqué the ribbon after the top row of patches has been assembled.

You might want to consider using gold lamé fabric in place of the yellow print for the angel's halo. Test the lamé fabric carefully to determine if it can be pressed with a warm iron. (If not, use your fingers to press seam allowances that include lamé.) Some quiltmakers prefer to fuse lamé to a lightweight interfacing before cutting it.

# Mary and Baby Jesus

**mother and child**

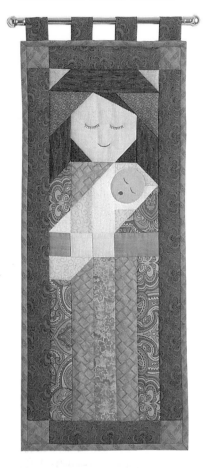

## Cutting Requirements
**Finished size:** 11¼" x 26¼"

| Ydg. | Fabric | Use | Cut |
|---|---|---|---|
| ⅛ yd. | Purple Print | borders, tabs | 2 N, 2 F, 4 P |
| ¼ yd. | Gold Print | binding, border corners | 1½" x 83", 4 A |
| ⅛ yd. | Light Blue Print | background | 2 LL |
| ¼ yd. | Flesh | Mary's face and hands | 1 MM, 2 A |
| ⅛ yd. | Flesh | Jesus' face | 1 Jesus' face |
| ⅛ yd. | Brown Print | hair | 1 C, 2 LL |
| ⅛ yd. | Medium Blue Print | veil | 1 PP, 1 S, 1 Sr |
| ⅛ yd. | Light Blue Print | veil | 2 SS |
| ⅛ yd. | Multi Print | garment | 1 Sr, 1 SS, 1 L, 1 M |
| ⅛ yd. | Light Blue Solid | garment sleeves | 1 A, 1 B |
| ⅛ yd. | Dusty Pink Print | garment | 1 SS, 1 FF, 1 M |
| ⅛ yd. | Bright Pink Print | garment center | 1 M |
| ⅛ yd. | White Print | Jesus' swaddling clothes | 1 LL, 1 DD, 1 EEr |
| ⅛ yd. | Off-White Print | Jesus' swaddling clothes | 2 EE, 1 EEr, 1 LL |
| ½ yd. | Light Solid | lining | 15" x 30" |

**Also Needed:**

| | |
|---|---|
| Blue floss | eyes |
| Red floss | mouths |

## Assembly

**1** Lay out all patches as shown in the piecing diagram.

**2** Sew hair over face as follows. Fold brown print C patch in half lengthwise and press. As shown below, position and pin C on flesh MM. Trim C to match shape of MM. Baste hair in place, sewing ⅛" from edge.

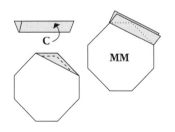

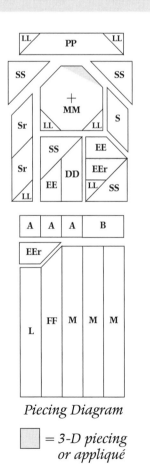

*Piecing Diagram*

□ = 3-D piecing or appliqué

34

**3** Join lettered patches as shown in the piecing diagram. Press seam allowances to one side. If dark seam allowances show through light fabric, trim seam allowances.

**4** Appliqué Jesus' face. Trim away behind appliqué to prevent show-through. Referring to information given at right, embroider Jesus' eyes in outline stitch and his mouth in satin stitch. Embroider Mary's mouth in outline stitch and her eyes in buttonhole stitch.

**5** Referring to the general instructions, add border strips and corner squares. Press seam allowances toward the borders.

**6** Referring to the general instructions, assemble lining, batting and quilt top. Quilt in-the-ditch as shown in the quilting diagram. Quilt next to Mary's eyes and mouth. Add tabs and bind the quilt.

## Embroidery Tips

**1.** Use 2 ply embroidery floss for Jesus' face. Use 2 or 3 ply for Mary's face.

**2.** Mark the design lightly with a sharp pencil. To do this, fold Mary's face patch in half lengthwise and crosswise to find the center. Align the center folds with the "Patch Center" given on the pattern and trace the eyes and mouth. (If you can't see through the fabric, tape the pattern to a window and hold the patch over the pattern. Light shining through the pattern will make it easier to trace.) For Jesus, you can trace the outline of the face patch and the embroidery design at the same time. Remember to add ³⁄₁₆" turn-under allowance outside the marked outline when cutting the patch.

**3.** After appliquéing Jesus' face, cut away the pieced "swaddling clothes" behind the patch *before* doing the embroidery.

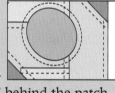

**4.** Be sure the floss "tails" are caught under the embroidery so they won't show through the face fabric.

*Patch Center*

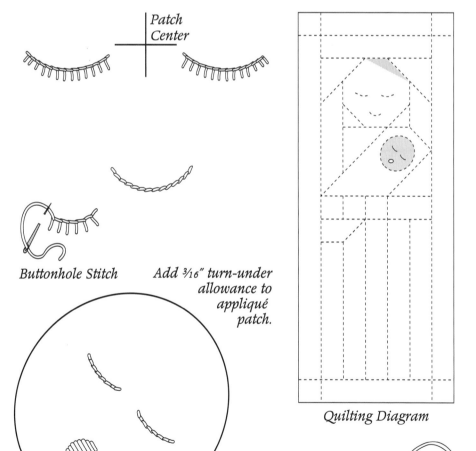

*Buttonhole Stitch*

*Add ³⁄₁₆" turn-under allowance to appliqué patch.*

*Quilting Diagram*

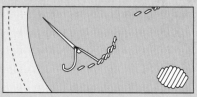

*Satin Stitch*     *Outline Stitch*

# Joseph

**went with Mary to Bethlehem**

## Cutting Requirements

**Finished size:** 11¼" x 26¼"

| Ydg. | Fabric | Use | Cut |
|------|--------|-----|-----|
| ⅛ yd. | Purple Print | borders, tabs | 2 N, 2 F, 4 P |
| ¼ yd. | Gold Print | binding, border corners | 1½" x 83", 4 A |
| ⅛ yd. | Light Blue Print | background | 1 EE, 1 EEr |
| ¼ yd. | Flesh | face and hand | 1 MM, 1 A |
| ⅛ yd. | Gray Print | hair, mustache, beard | 2 LL, 1 mustache, 1 S, 1 Sr, 1 B |
| ⅛ yd. | Multi/Rust Print | headdress, garment center | 1 D, 1 K |
| ¼ yd. | Brown Stripe | headdress | 1 KK, 1 KKr |
| ⅛ yd. | Turquoise Print | garment | 1 EE, 1 EEr, 1 Z, 1 Zr |
| ⅛ yd. | Turquoise Print | garment sleeves | 1AA, 1 AAr |
| ⅛ yd. | Light Green Print | garment sleeves | 1 Z, 1 Zr |
| ⅛ yd. | Green Plaid | garment | 2 LL, 1 Y, 1 Yr |
| ½ yd. | Light Solid | lining | 15" x 30" |

## Assembly

**1** Lay out all patches as shown in the piecing diagram.

**2** Join lettered patches as shown in the piecing diagram. Press seam allowances to one side.

**3** Appliqué Joseph's mustache. Appliqué eyes unless they will be made with buttons.

**4** Referring to the general instructions, add border strips and corner squares. Press seam allowances toward the borders.

**5** Referring to the general instructions, assemble lining, batting and quilt top. Quilt in-the-ditch as shown in the quilting diagram. Add tabs and bind the quilt.

**6** Add button eyes if they were not appliquéd.

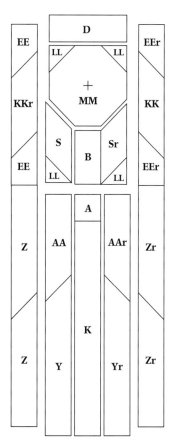

*Piecing Diagram*

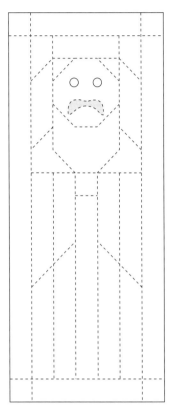

*Quilting Diagram*

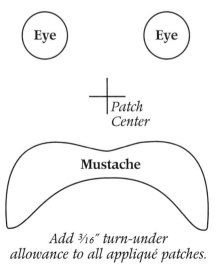

Eye          Eye

┼ *Patch*
*Center*

**Mustache**

*Add ³⁄₁₆″ turn-under*
*allowance to all appliqué patches.*

## Proud Parents

Joseph and Mary can be combined to make a quilt that finishes 24¾″ x 29¼″.

**1.** Make the two quilt tops as explained in project directions.

**2.** Cut 2 strips 2″ x 26″ and 2 strips 2″ x 21½″. Cut 4 A patches. Cut binding 1½″ x 116″. Cut lining 29″ x 33″. Cut batting 29″ x 33″.

**3.** Join the quilt tops. Sew long borders to sides. Press seam allowances toward borders. Sew an A square to each end of short border strip for top border. Repeat to make bottom border like this. Press seam allowances toward border strips. Sew borders to top and bottom of quilt.

**4.** Assemble lining, batting and quilt top as explained in the general instructions. Quilt, add tabs (if desired) and bind.

# Shepherd

**watches the flock by night**

## Cutting Requirements

**Finished size: 11¼" x 26¼"**

| Ydg. | Fabric | Use | Cut |
|---|---|---|---|
| ⅛ yd. | Green Print | borders, tabs | 2 N, 2 F, 4 P |
| ¼ yd. | Gold Print | binding, border corners | 1½" x 83", 4 A |
| ⅛ yd. | Dark Blue Print | background | 2 LL, 2 A, 1 EE, 1 EEr |
| ¼ yd. | Flesh | face and hands | 1 W, 2 A |
| ⅛ yd. | Brown Print | hair | 2 A |
| ⅛ yd. | Brown Print | sleeve cuff | 1 G |
| ⅛ yd. | Light Brown Print | headdress | 1 PP, 1 AA, 1 AAr |
| ¼ yd. | Brown Stripe | sleeves | 1 BB, 1 AAr |
| ¼ yd. | Brown Stripe | shepherd's staff | 1 each piece of staff |
| ⅜ yd. | Red Stripe | garment | 1 H, 1 G, 1 FF, 2 A |
| ⅛ yd. | Off-White Print | garment center | 1 M, 1 A |
| ⅛ yd. | White/Blue Print | lamb | 1 EEr, 1 O, 1 PP |
| ⅛ yd. | Black Solid | lamb's face, tail, legs | 1 face, 1 tail, 2 A |
| ½ yd. | Light Solid | lining | 15" x 30" |
| **Also Needed:** | | | |
| Red floss | | mouth | |

## Assembly

**1** Lay out all patches as shown in the piecing diagram.

**2** Sew hair over face as follows. Fold brown print A patch in half diagonally and press. Position A so that the square corners of triangle and the corner of flesh W match; pin in place. Repeat for other brown print A patch. Baste A triangles in place, sewing ⅛" from edge.

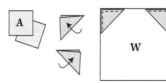

**3** Sew lamb's legs in place as follows. Fold black A patch in half; press. As shown on next page, position folded A on red

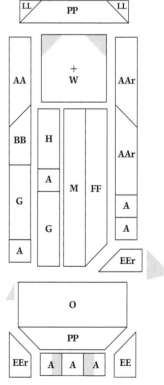

*Piecing Diagram*

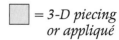 = 3-D piecing or appliqué

stripe A, matching raw edges. Baste leg in place. Repeat for other black and red stripe A

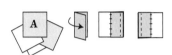

patches. Blindstitch folded edges to red stripe A patches.

4 Join lettered patches as shown in the piecing diagram. Wherever possible, press seam allowances toward the shepherd or lamb. If dark seam allowances show through light fabric, trim seam allowances.

5 Appliqué eyes if they will not be made with buttons. Embroider mouth.

6 Referring to the general instructions, add border strips and corner squares. Press seam allowances toward the borders.

7 To appliqué the lamb's face and tail, sew patches in place over border strips, opening the border seams and tucking in edges of patches before closing seams.

8 Appliqué the shepherd's staff, opening seams and tucking in ends before closing seams.

9 Referring to the general instructions, assemble lining, batting and quilt top. Quilt in-the-ditch as shown in the quilting diagram. Add tabs and bind the quilt.

10 Add buttons for eyes if they were not appliquéd.

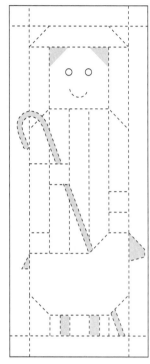

*Quilting Diagram*

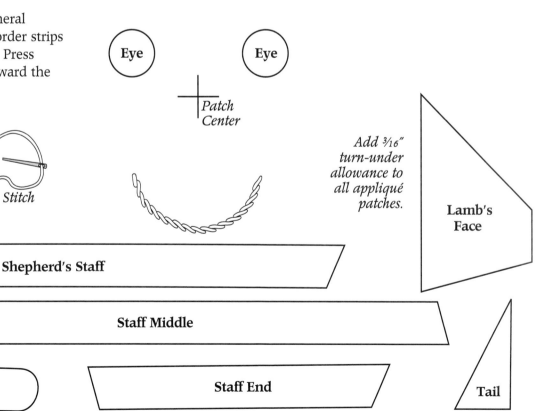

*Outline Stitch*

Eye    Eye

+
*Patch Center*

*Add ³⁄₁₆″ turn-under allowance to all appliqué patches.*

**Lamb's Face**

**Shepherd's Staff**

**Staff Middle**

**Staff End**

**Tail**

# King I

**King Caspar brings gold**

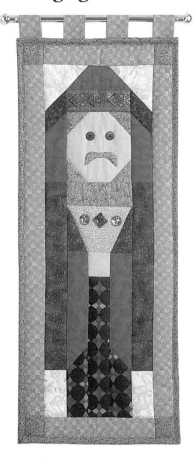

## Cutting Requirements

**Finished size:** 11¼" x 26¼"

| Ydg. | Fabric | Use | Cut |
|---|---|---|---|
| ⅛ yd. | Gold Print | borders, tabs | 2 N, 2 F, 4 P |
| ¼ yd. | Turquoise Print | binding, border corners | 1½" x 83", 4 A |
| ⅛ yd. | Beige Print | background | 2 SS, 2 B |
| ⅛ yd. | Magenta Print | headdress, sleeves | 1 II, 1 D, 1 DD, 1 DDr, 1 Z, 1 Zr |
| ⅛ yd. | Purple Print | headdress | 1 JJ, 1 JJr |
| ⅛ yd. | Gray Print | hair, beard, mustache | 4 LL, 1 D, 1 mustache |
| ¼ yd. | Flesh Print | face, hand | 1 MM, 1 A |
| ⅛ yd. | Green Print | robe | 2 K, 1 T, 1 Tr |
| ⅛ yd. | Navy/Multi Print | robe | 1 DD, 1 DDr, 1 L |
| ⅛ yd. | Gold Print | gold | 1 UU |
| ½ yd. | Light Solid | lining | 15" x 30" |
| **Also Needed:** | | | |
| 5" of 1½"-wide braid | | headdress trim | |

## Creative Options

**Eyes:** use ⅝" buttons *or* appliqué circle patches
**Headdress:** add elegant braid trim
**Gold:** add rhinestone button jewels *or* appliqué jewel patches

## Assembly

**1** Lay out all patches as shown in the piecing diagram.

**2** Join lettered patches as shown in the piecing diagram. Note: After sewing the magenta D patch to the top of the head, appliqué braid over D. The ends of the braid will be caught in the seams when other pieces are added.

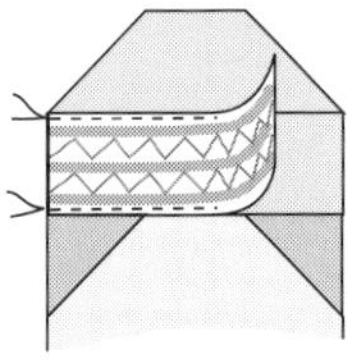

Wherever possible, press seam allowances toward king and away from the background.

**3** Appliqué mustache. Appliqué eyes and jewels unless they will be done with buttons and 3-D jewels.

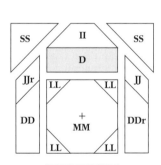
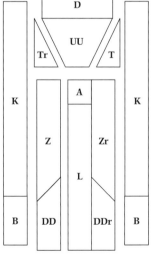

*Piecing Diagram*

☐ = 3-D piecing or appliqué

**4** Referring to the general instructions, add border strips and corner squares. Press seam allowances toward the borders.

**5** Referring to the general instructions, assemble lining, batting and quilt top. Quilt in-the-ditch as shown in the quilting diagram. Add tabs and bind the quilt.

**6** (optional) Add buttons for eyes and jewels if they were not appliquéd.

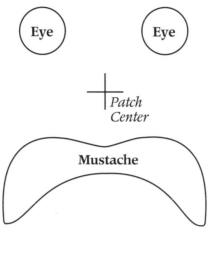

Eye     Eye

*Patch Center*

**Mustache**

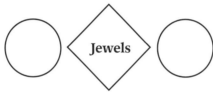

**Jewels**

*Add ³⁄₁₆″ turn-under allowance to all appliqué patches.*

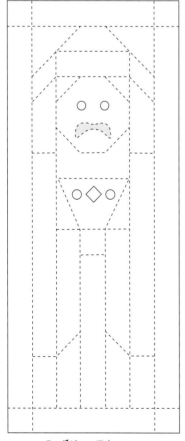

*Quilting Diagram*

## Regal Trim Tips

It's amazing how a little elegant trim and a few sparkly faceted buttons can add a lot to make a king look truly regal. Here are a few tips to assure success for your project.

✧ When choosing braid trim, look at the label to see if it can be pressed safely. Some metallic threads could melt under a hot iron. If the trim you choose should not be pressed with an iron, simply use your fingers to press the seam allowances that are close to the trim.

✧ Some trims ravel very easily. If you can see that this might be a problem, sew a line of zigzag stitching at each end of the piece of trim to be sure it does not disappear before your eyes.

✧ When sewing on the button jewels, you can use thread to match the button or you might want to use metallic gold thread for a little extra twinkle.

# King II

King Melchior
brings frankincense

## Creative Options

**Crown:** add rhinestone button jewels *or* appliqué jewel patches
**Eyes:** use ⅝" buttons *or* appliqué circle patches

## Cutting Requirements

**Finished size:** 11¼" x 26¼"

| Ydg. | Fabric | Use | Cut |
|------|--------|-----|-----|
| ⅛ yd. | Turquoise Print | borders, tabs | 2 N, 2 F, 4 P |
| ¼ yd. | Gold Print | binding, border corners | 1½" x 83", 4 A |
| ⅛ yd. | Beige Print | background | 1 AA, 1 AAr, 1 T, 1 Tr |
| ⅛ yd. | Gold Print | crown | 1 XX |
| ⅛ yd. | Yellow Print | crown trim, frankincense | 4 A, 1 II |
| ¼ yd. | Flesh Print | face, hand | 1 W, 1 A |
| ⅛ yd. | Gray Print | hair | 2 A |
| ⅛ yd. | Purple Print | upper robe | 1 PP, 1 EE, 1 EEr |
| ¼ yd. | Red Stripe | sleeves | 1 Z, 1 Zr |
| ¼ yd. | Black/Purple Stripe | sleeves | 1 AA, 1 AAr |
| ⅛ yd. | Red Print | center and bottom of robe | 2 F |
| ⅛ yd. | Blue Print | lower robe | 1 DD, 1 DDr, 1 AA, 1 AAr |
| ½ yd. | Light Solid | lining | 15" x 30" |
| **Also Needed:** | | | |
| Red floss | | mouth | |

## Assembly

**1** Lay out all patches as shown in the piecing diagram.

**2** Prepare trim for crown as follows. As shown below, fold yellow print patch A in half diagonally and press. Fold in half again diagonally; press. Repeat for two more yellow print A patches. Position folded patches on XX crown patch as shown below; baste them in place, sewing ⅛" from edge.

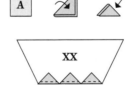

**3** Sew hair over face as follows. Fold gray print patch A in half diagonally and press as shown on next page. Position A so that the square corner of tri-

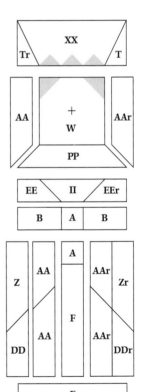

*Piecing Diagram*

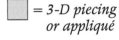 = 3-D piecing or appliqué

angle and the corner of flesh W match; pin in place. Repeat for other gray print A patch. Baste A triangles in place.

4 Join lettered patches as shown in the piecing diagram. Wherever possible, press seam allowances toward king and away from the background.

5 Referring to the general instructions, add border strips and corner squares. Press seam allowances toward the borders.

6 Embroider mouth with red embroidery floss. Appliqué jewel patches to crown and appliqué eyes (optional). If desired, put a small amount of polyester batting under appliqués for puffiness.

7 Referring to the general instructions, assemble lining, batting and quilt top. Quilt in-the-ditch as shown in the quilting diagram. Add tabs and bind the quilt.

8 (optional) Add buttons for eyes; sew rhinestone jewels to crown if they were not appliquéd. Tack points of crown trim triangles in place, adding beads or small jewels if desired.

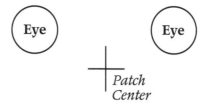

Patch Center

*Outline Stitch*

**Jewel**

*Add ³⁄₁₆" turn-under allowance to all appliqué patches.*

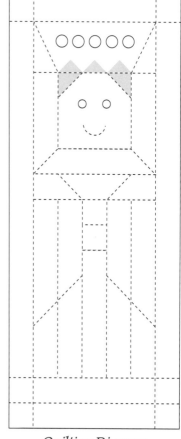

*Quilting Diagram*

# King III

## King Balthazar brings myrrh

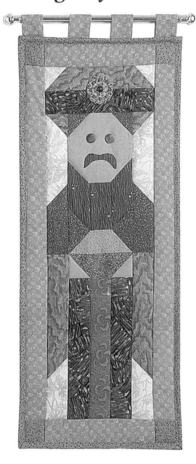

## Cutting Requirements

**Finished size:** 11¼" x 26¼"

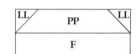

| Ydg. | Fabric | Use | Cut |
|------|--------|-----|-----|
| ⅛ yd. | Gold Print | borders, tabs | 2 N, 2 F, 4 P |
| ¼ yd. | Turquoise Print | binding, border corners | 1½" x 83", 4 A |
| ⅛ yd. | Beige Print | background | 2 LL, 2 TT, 1 BB, 1 BBr |
| ⅛ yd. | Purple Print | turban, sleeves | 1 PP, 2 LL, 1 CC, 1 CCr |
| ⅛ yd. | Multi Print | turban, robe | 1 F, 2 L |
| ⅛ yd. | Violet Print | turban, upper robe | 2 LL, 1 DD, 1 DDr, 2 OO |
| ⅛ yd. | Violet Print | center of robe | 1 L |
| ¼ yd. | Flesh Print | face, hand | 1 MM, 2 LL |
| ⅛ yd. | Rust Print | mustache, beard | 1 mustache, 1 S, 1 Sr, 1 B |
| ⅛ yd. | Gold Print | top part of myrrh | 1 II |
| ⅛ yd. | Dark Gold Print | bottom part of myrrh | 1 II |
| ½ yd. | Light Solid | lining | 15" x 30" |

## Assembly

**1** Lay out all patches as shown in the piecing diagram.

**2** Join lettered patches as shown in the piecing diagram. Wherever possible, press seam allowances toward king and away from the background.

**3** Appliqué mustache patch. (optional) Appliqué eyes.

**4** Referring to the general instructions, add border strips and corner squares. Press seam allowances toward the borders.

**5** Referring to the general instructions, assemble lining, batting and quilt top. Quilt in-the-ditch as shown in the quilting diagram. Add tabs and bind the quilt.

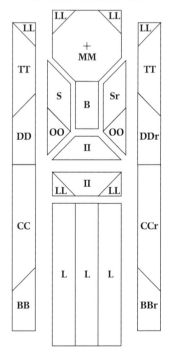

*Piecing Diagram*

**6** (optional) Add buttons for eyes if they were not appliquéd. Sew medallion appliqué and/or feathers to turban.

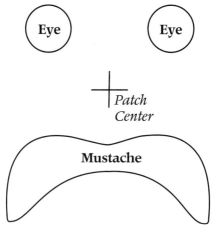

Eye          Eye

╋ *Patch Center*

**Mustache**

*Add ³⁄₁₆" turn-under allowance to all appliqué patches.*

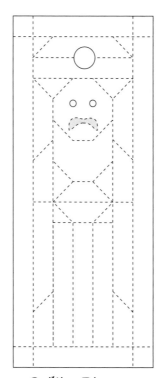

*Quilting Diagram*

## We Three Kings

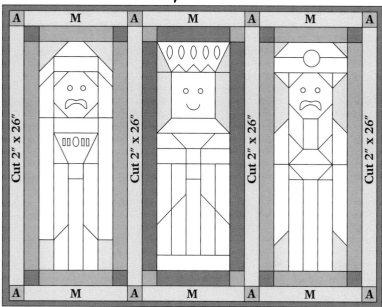

The Three Kings can be combined to make a quilt that finishes 38¼" x 29¼".

**1.** Make the three quilt tops as explained in the project directions.

**2.** Cut 4 strips 2" x 26" and 6 M strips. Cut 8 A patches. Cut binding 1½" x 143". Cut lining 42" x 33". Cut batting 42" x 33".

**3.** Join the quilt tops alternately with the long strips.

Press the seam allowances toward the strips. Join 4 A squares alternately with 3 M strips to make the top border. Repeat to make the bottom border like this. Press the seam allowances toward the M strips. Sew borders to the top and bottom edges of the quilt.

**4.** Assemble lining, batting and quilt top as explained in the general instructions. Quilt, add tabs (if desired) and bind.

# Patterns A-I

Patterns appear in
alphabetical order
and tend to be
grouped by shape.

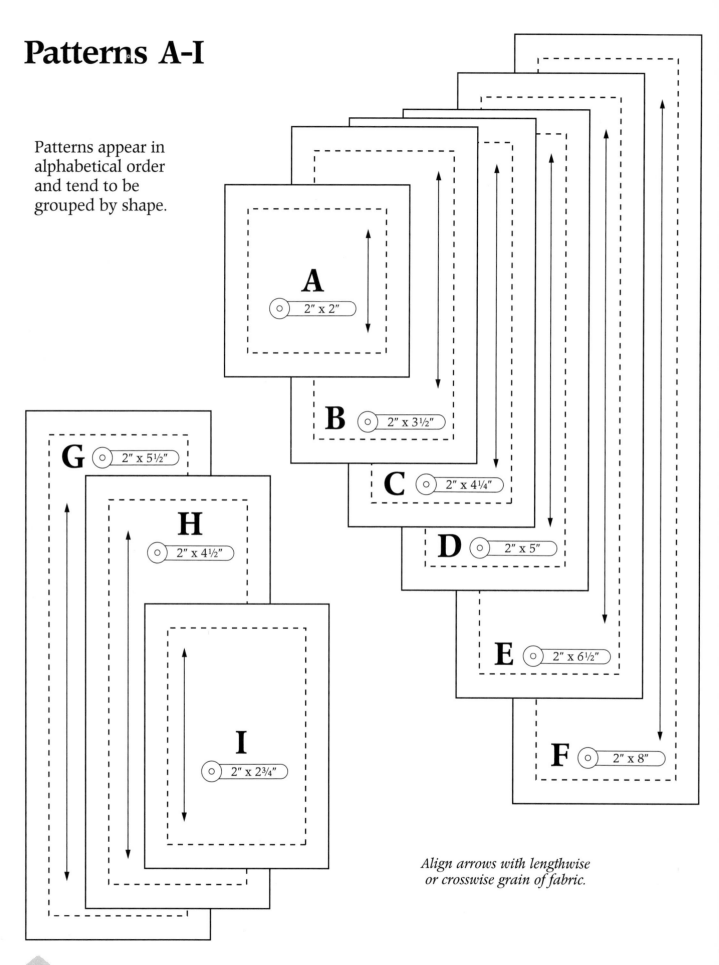

**A**
2″ x 2″

**B**
2″ x 3½″

**C**
2″ x 4¼″

**D**
2″ x 5″

**E**
2″ x 6½″

**F**
2″ x 8″

**G**
2″ x 5½″

**H**
2″ x 4½″

**I**
2″ x 2¾″

*Align arrows with lengthwise
or crosswise grain of fabric.*

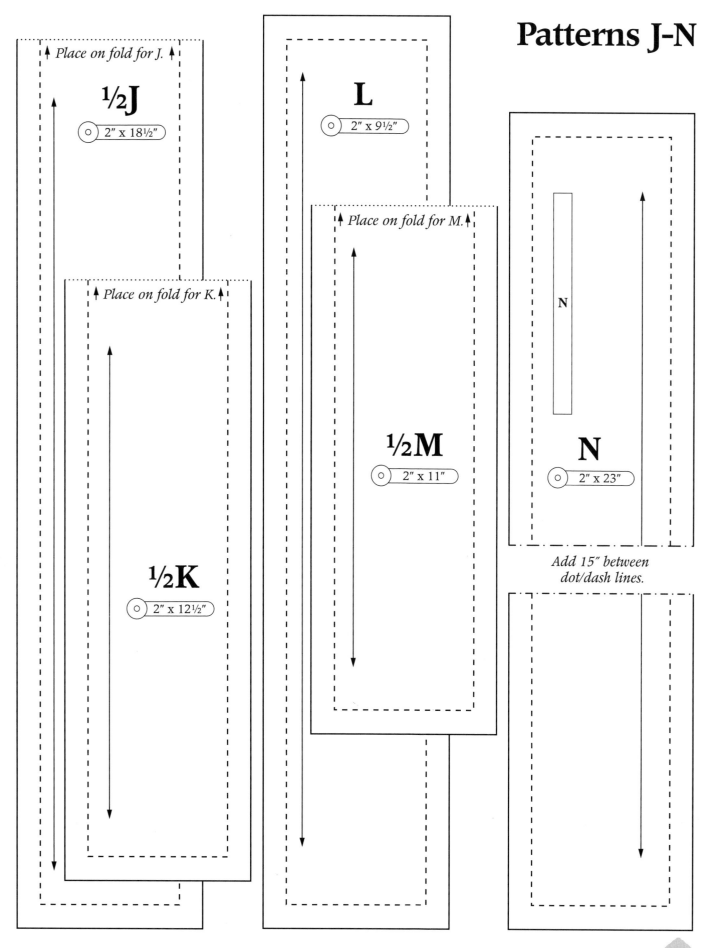

# Patterns J-N

*Place on fold for J.*

## ½J

2" x 18½"

## L

2" x 9½"

*Place on fold for K.*

*Place on fold for M.*

N

## ½K

2" x 12½"

## ½M

2" x 11"

## N

2" x 23"

*Add 15" between dot/dash lines.*

# Patterns O-S

*Align arrows with lengthwise
or crosswise grain of fabric.*

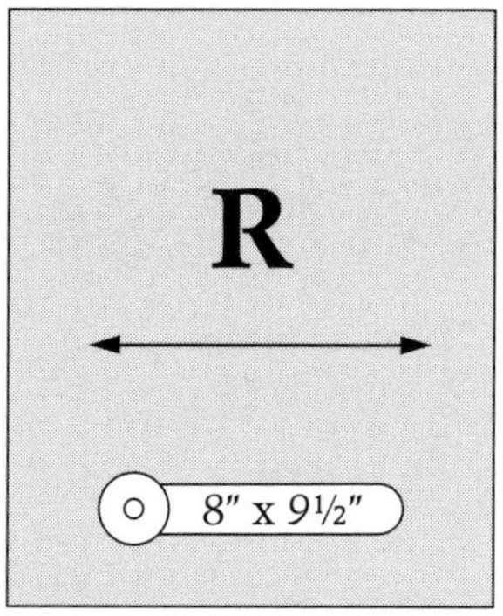

**R**

8" x 9½"

*Dimensions of diagramed patch
include seam allowances.
Cut size as given.*

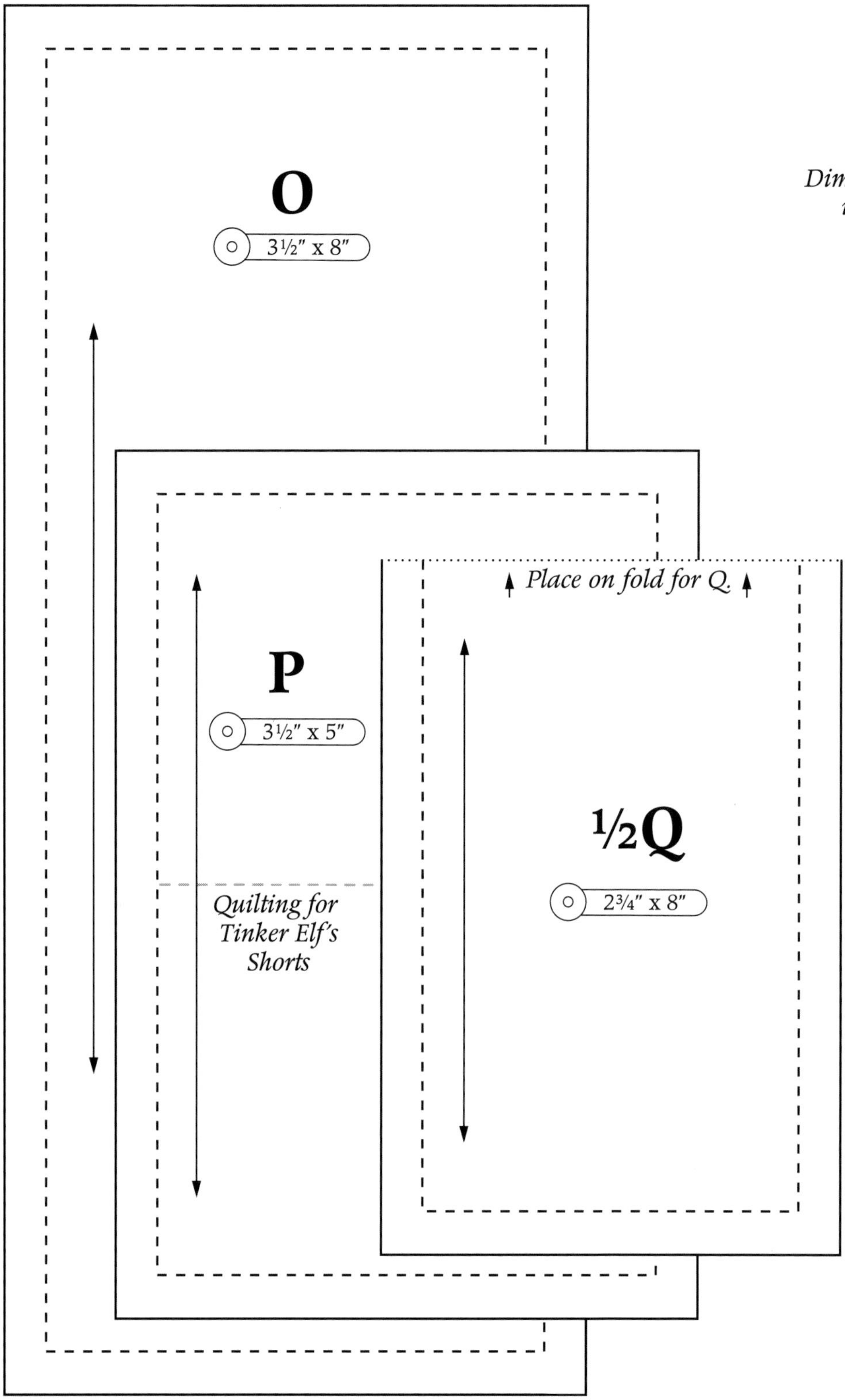

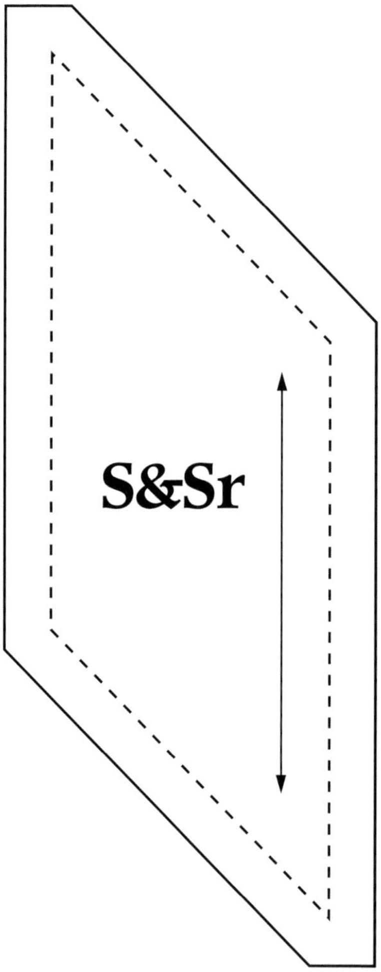

**O**

3½" x 8"

**P**

3½" x 5"

*Place on fold for Q.*

*Quilting for
Tinker Elf's
Shorts*

**½Q**

2¾" x 8"

**S&Sr**

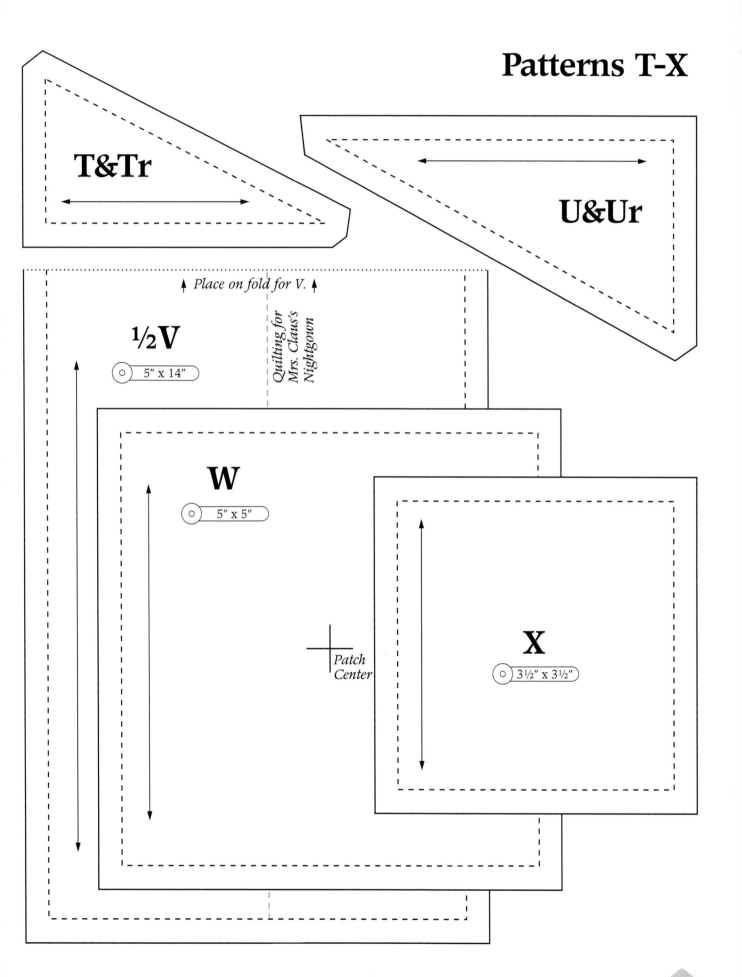

**T&Tr**

**U&Ur**

*Place on fold for V.*

½**V**

5" x 14"

*Quilting for Mrs. Claus's Nightgown*

**W**

5" x 5"

+ *Patch Center*

**X**

3½" x 3½"

# Patterns Y-BB

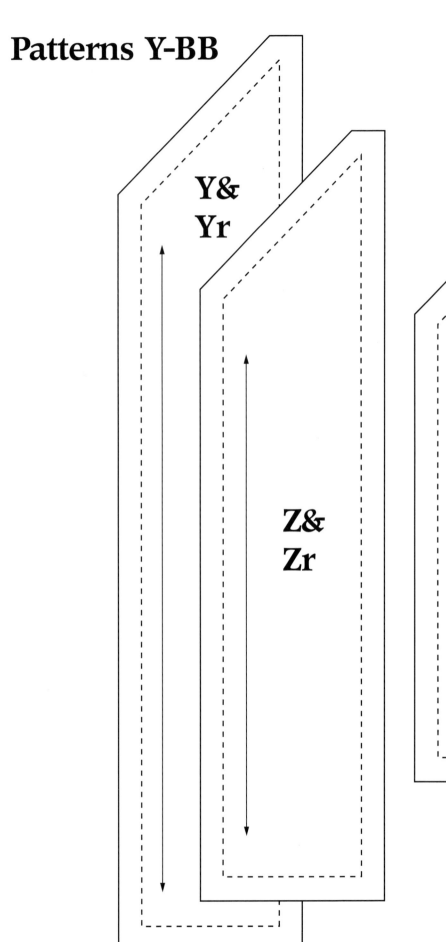

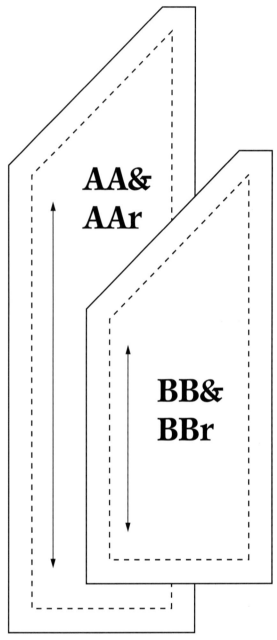

Y&
Yr

Z&
Zr

AA&
AAr

BB&
BBr

*Align arrows with lengthwise
or crosswise grain of fabric.*

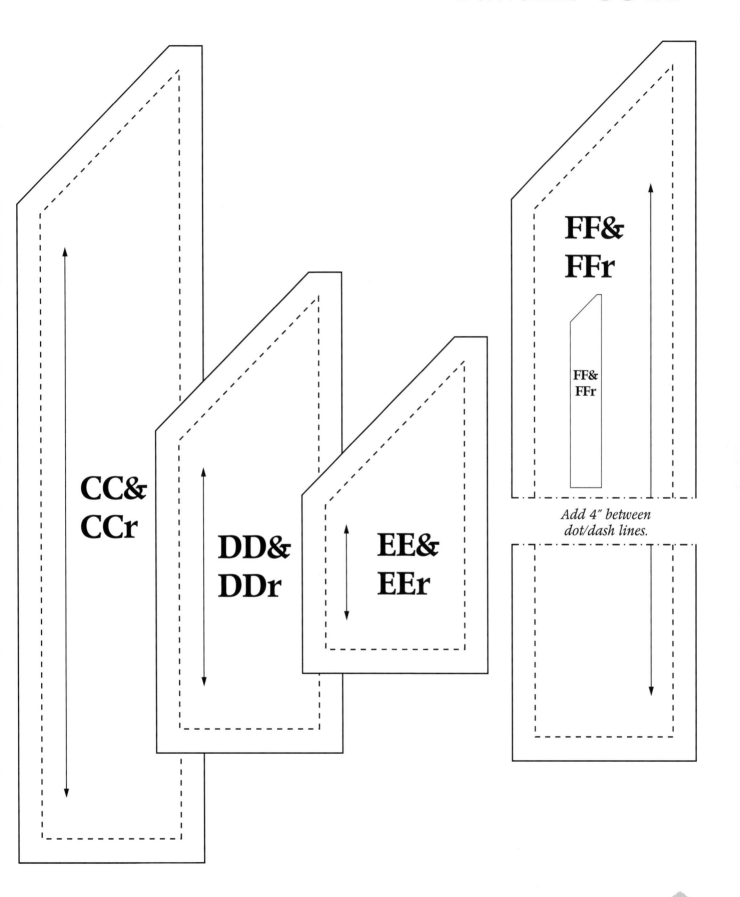

CC&
CCr

DD&
DDr

EE&
EEr

FF&
FFr

FF&
FFr

*Add 4" between dot/dash lines.*

# Patterns GG-LL

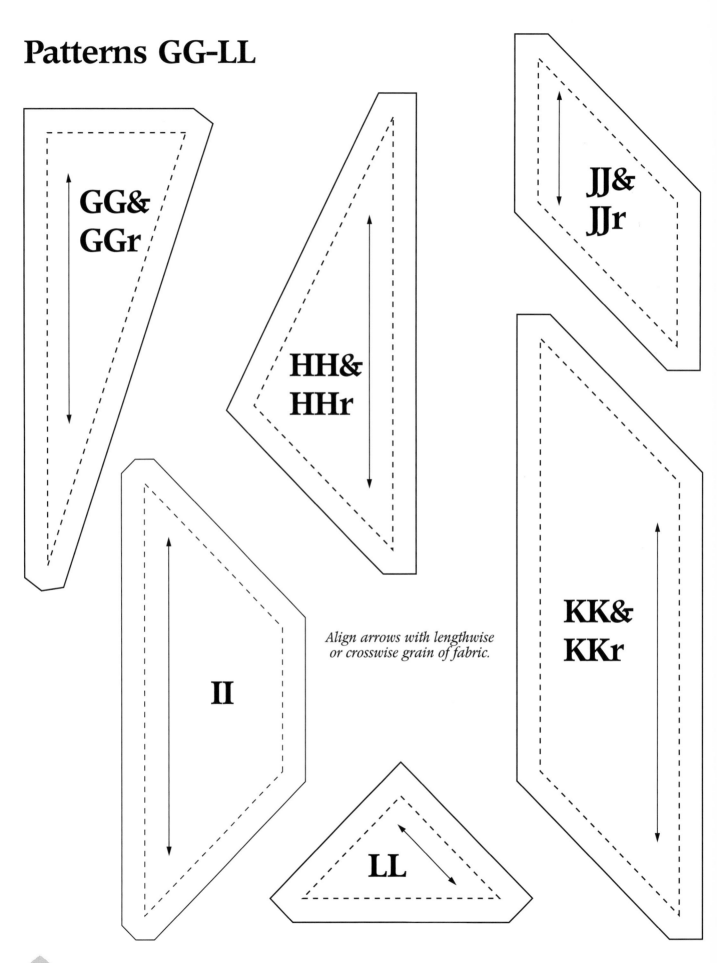

GG&
GGr

HH&
HHr

JJ&
JJr

II

KK&
KKr

*Align arrows with lengthwise
or crosswise grain of fabric.*

LL

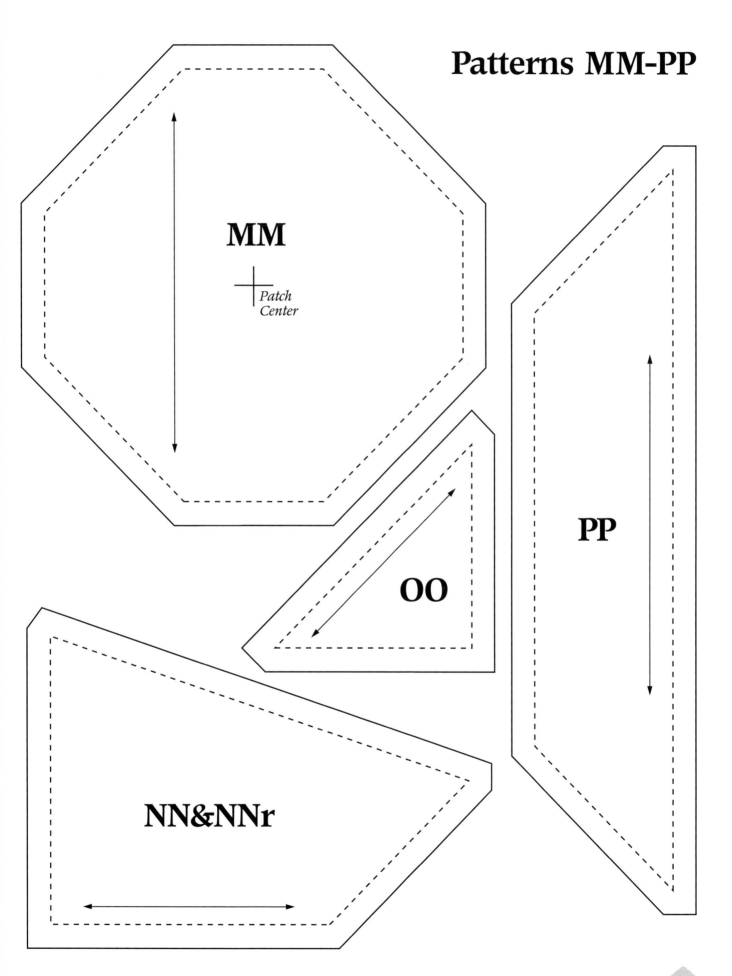

MM

Patch Center

OO

NN&NNr

PP

# Patterns QQ-VV

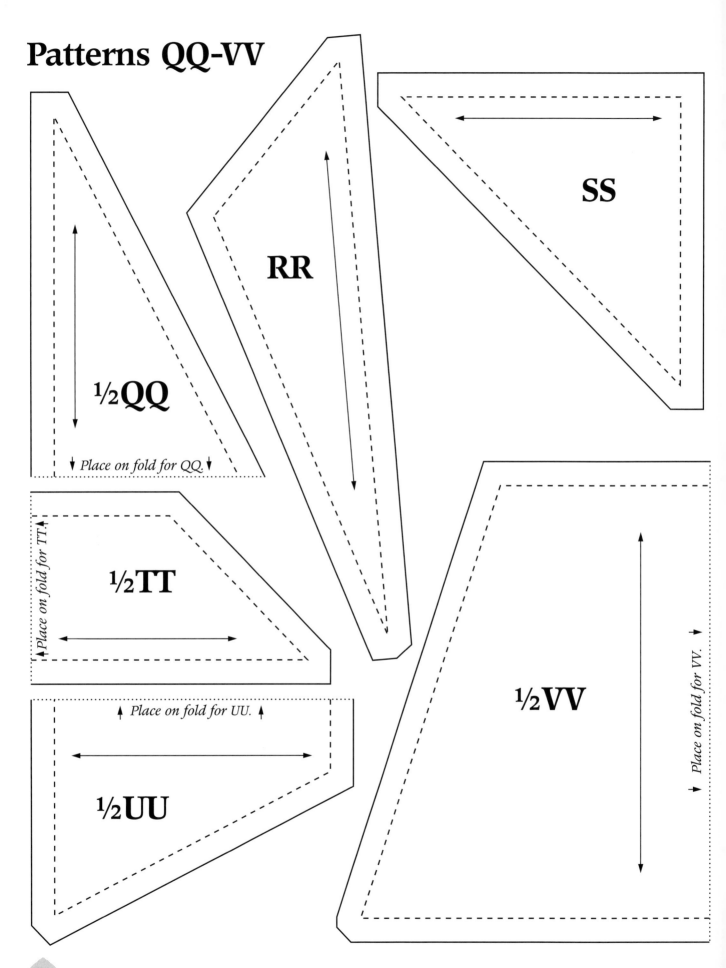

½QQ

*Place on fold for QQ.*

RR

SS

*Place on fold for TT.*

½TT

*Place on fold for UU.*

½UU

½VV

*Place on fold for VV.*

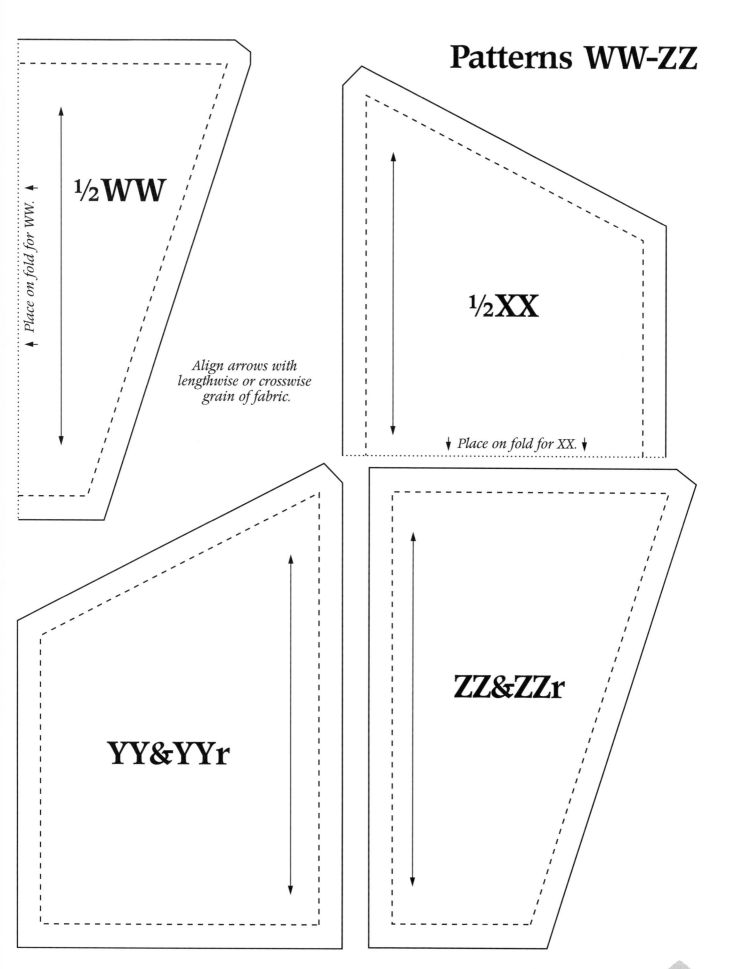

½WW

Place on fold for WW.

Align arrows with lengthwise or crosswise grain of fabric.

½XX

Place on fold for XX.

YY&YYr

ZZ&ZZr

# General Instructions

This section covers the basic information you will need to make the quilts in this book. It will be especially helpful to beginning quiltmakers, but even those who have sewn quilts for many years may benefit from a quick refresher course. The information is given in the same order as quilts are made, so you will easily be able to find answers to specific questions as they arise. Don't forget that special techniques are explained on pages 4 and 5.

## About Sizes

All the quilts in this book measure the same size. To help you check your sewing as you proceed, here are the *finished (sewn)* sizes for the quilts.
Design block: 7½" x 22½"
Borders: 1½" wide
Binding: ⅜" wide
Completed quilt: 11¼" x 26¼" plus tabs

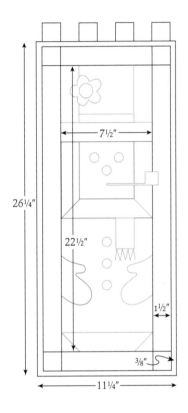

## Selecting Fabrics

For many quilters, fabric selection is one of the most fun steps of quiltmaking. Of course, you are welcome to try to match the photos to select fabrics that are very close or identical to those used in the original quilts. The fabrics we selected were all readily available at the time we chose them, and none were especially unique or rare. We can also say that there were countless other combinations of fabrics that would have been successful.

While selection of fabrics need not be difficult or mysterious, there are a few points that will help.

**Skin Tones:** We used solid cotton fabrics for all skin tones. Shades range from light pink through various peaches to medium brown. Choose colors that look right to you.

**Hair:** As with skin tones, you can select hair colors as you wish. The Elves could have blond hair instead of brown, Mary could have black hair, and Mrs. Claus could have red hair instead of her blue-gray "rinse." We chose prints for all hair, mustaches and beards.

**Novelty Fabrics:** Although cotton fabrics are the traditional choice for quilts, we chose felt for Santa's beard and mustache, we used pink satin for the Sugar Plum Fairy's ballet slippers, and we chose black satin for the Nutcracker and Santa. When choosing novelty fabrics, look for those that will not stretch and which are about the same weight as cotton. Suggestions include a lightweight brocade for the Kings' robes, lamé for the Heavenly Angel's halo, lightweight corduroy for the Elf outfits, and flannel for the Snowman's body and scarf. Mrs. Claus would look warm and comfy in a flannel nightie. If your quilts will ever be washed, of course you will want to choose washable fabrics.

**Contrast:** To make the figures distinct, it is important that the skin, hair, clothing and other design elements contrast with the background and with each other. For example, our first selection for the Elves skin was too light and did not contrast sufficiently with the background. So we chose a slightly darker (ruddier) peach fabric for the skin. When selecting fabrics, stand back several feet and squint to check the contrast. It will also be helpful to collect more than one option (especially since the yardage amounts are small) and try more than one fabric as you are cutting and sewing.

It is your choice whether or not to wash fabrics before cutting them. Many quilt books offer opinions about the pros and cons of prewashing fabric. It is always a good idea to test fabrics individually to see if the color will run. It's also a good idea to lightly spray fabric with water and iron it, both to get the folds out of it and to allow fabric to shrink somewhat.

## Cutting Patches

All straight-edged patches can easily be cut with a rotary cutter. Dimensions are given on square and rectangular pattern pieces, so you can simply use those measurements instead of tracing and cutting patterns.

2" x 5½"

For all other straight-edged shapes, trace patterns (or photocopy them if you have access to an accurate copier) and cut them out. Place patterns face up on right side of fabric, position a rotary-cutting ruler along the edge of the pattern, and cut. For patterns marked with an "r," which means "reversed," place pattern face down on right side of fabric before cutting.

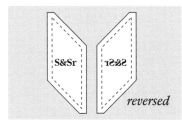

*reversed*

If you prefer, you can cut patches with scissors. To use scissors, you can either mark around patterns and cut on marked lines, or you can pin the pattern to the fabric and cut around the pattern without marking.

Patterns for appliqué pieces do not include turn-under allowances. Trace or copy these patterns and cut them out to make templates. Place template face up on right side of fabric and mark around it with a pencil. Add ³⁄₁₆" turn-under allowance (outside the marked lines) when cutting fabrics, judging this distance by eye. Appliqué patches are cut with scissors instead of a rotary cutter. For 3-D appliqué patches, mark one pattern shape on the wrong side of fabric. Then place another layer of fabric (right sides touching) under the marked fabric and cut both layers at one

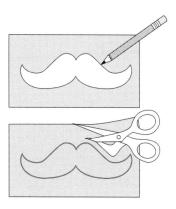

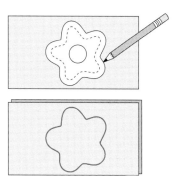

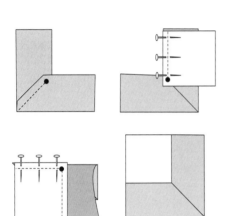

time. Leave these pairs of patches together so they are ready for sewing.

## Piecing

Machine piecing is ideal for these quilts. Use a neutral-color thread (such as a medium beige or gray) if you prefer not to change thread colors for various fabrics.

As for all machine piecing, there are two important points to keep in mind. First, be sure your seam allowances are an accurate ¼" width to assure that all pieces will fit well. Second, whenever a patch has an angled or "set-in" seam such as the example shown at left, begin or end the line of sewing exactly at the seam line, not at the edge of the patch. The seam that forms the adjacent part of the angle will begin at exactly the same point. Find more information about set-in seams on page 27.

## Appliqué

Appliqué patches are sewn after the piecing is finished, except in the case of patches that are partially included in a seam. One example is Frosty the Snowman's mittens. Because the straight edges of the mittens are enclosed in the border seams, the mittens should be appliquéd to Frosty's body before adding the borders.

To do hand appliqué, place the marked and cut patch face up on the quilt top. Baste it in place or use one or two pins to hold it. Use a single strand of thread that matches the appliqué (not the background); tie a small knot in the end of the thread. Turn under the allowance with the point of the needle and sew just inside the marked line with a blind stitch.

Stitches should be about ⅛" apart and most likely will not show.

Clip turn-under allowances on inside (concave) curves.

End the line of sewing with a couple of small backstitches. Trim away the background behind the appliqué if it will show through. It will probably not be necessary to trim away behind mustaches, but you will want to trim away behind Jesus' face on the Mary quilt.

## Adding Borders & Corner Squares

All the quilts in this book have long borders (N), short borders (F) and corner squares (A). After completing the quilt design block, you will be ready to add borders and corner squares.

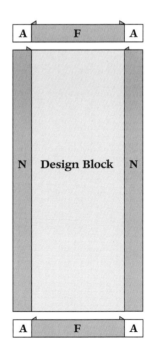

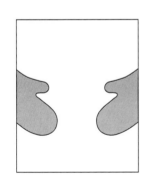

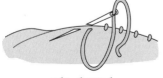

*Blind Stitch*

Sew long borders to sides of quilt top. Press seam allowances toward borders. Sew corner squares to ends of short borders. Press seam allowances toward short borders. Sew a short border/corner square to the upper edge of the quilt top; repeat for the bottom edge. Press seam allowances toward borders.

## Assembling the Layers & Quilting

Check the quilt top to be sure that dark threads or seam allowances do not show through. If necessary, give the quilt top a final pressing.

Cut lining 15″ x 30″. Press lining to eliminate creases or wrinkles. Spread lining on a table; tape it in place (optional). Cut batting to be 15″ x 30″ and lay it on top of the lining. Smooth any wrinkles. Center quilt top over batting. Use straight pins to hold the layers together. Baste the layers together, either with running stitches (about 1″ to 2″ long) or hold the layers together with small safety pins. Avoid basting along seams that will be quilted. You will find quilting diagrams with the project directions. Also baste ⅛″ from the edge of the quilt top (with running stitches, not pins). This basting can remain after the quilting is finished to make it easier to do the binding.

Working either by hand or by machine, quilt in-the-ditch as shown in the quilting diagram. To quilt in-the-ditch, sew along the seam line on the "low" side of the seam, which is the side without seam allowances. Quilting in-the-ditch around appliqués will make those patches puff up a bit. Add other quilting as you wish.

## Adding Tabs & Binding the Quilt

To prepare the quilt for adding tabs and binding, trim lining and batting to extend *beyond the quilt top by ⅛″*. This will allow a finished binding width of ⅜″.

Prepare tabs by folding P patches in half lengthwise with right sides together. Sew with a ¼″ seam and turn right side out. Press flat, either with the seam centered or at one edge. Repeat to make four tabs.

Fold tabs in half so raw edges match. Working on the back side of the quilt, position and pin four tabs evenly spaced across the upper edge of the quilt. The outer two tabs should align with the corner squares and will be ⅜″ from the edges of the lining. The binding will be sewn over the raw edges of the tabs.

The instructions for each quilt project call for binding 1½″ x 83″. Depending on the width of your fabric, you will need to cut either two or three 1½″-wide strips across the width of the fabric. Join strips end-to-end; press seam allowances open.

The binding can either be sewn to the front of the quilt and turned to the back side, or it can be sewn to the back side and turned to the front. The quilts shown in this book were done with both options. The illustrations show the binding sewn to the front side and folded to the back side.

Cut the beginning of the binding strip at a 45° angle. Fold edge in ¼″ and press. Working on a table and starting on one long side of quilt (not at a corner), pin right side of binding to quilt top. Be careful not to stretch the edge

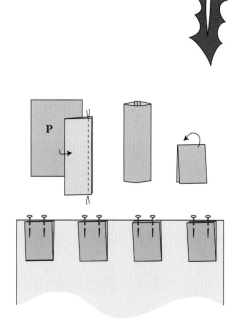

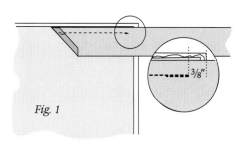

*Fig. 1*

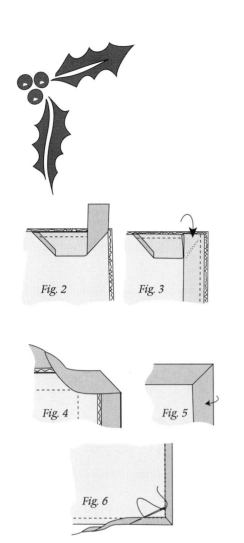

Fig. 2  Fig. 3

Fig. 4  Fig. 5

Fig. 6

of the quilt. Machine stitch (through all layers) ⅜" from edge of the lining (or ¼" from the edge of the quilt top), stopping the line of sewing ⅜" from the next edge of the lining. Backstitch; cut threads. (Fig. 1)

Lay the quilt flat on a table. Fold the binding strip away from the quilt (Fig. 2), then fold it down again to position the binding strip along the next edge of the quilt (Fig. 3). Pin binding in place. Stitch from the fold of the binding along this edge, again stopping ⅜" from next edge. Repeat this procedure until the binding has been sewn all around the quilt. Overlap ends and cut off any excess binding.

Turn the binding to the other side of the quilt and fold under the ⅜" seam allowance. Pin the folded edge in place, just covering the first line of sewing. At each corner, fold binding in the sequence shown to make a miter.

(Figs. 4 and 5)

Sew the folded edge in place by either of two methods. You can use hand-sewn blind stitching and thread to match the binding. (Fig. 6) Or you can use machine zigzag stitching that just catches the edge of the binding. Use invisible thread (on top) and thread to match the binding (in the bobbin). Either way, this stitching should also catch the tabs to hold them extending up and away from the quilt.

## Adding a Label

It's always a nice touch to make and add a label. One easy way to make a label is to enlarge the drawing of your quilt (from the inside back cover) and trace it on muslin with a Pigma™ permanent pen. Sign your name, the name of the quilt, and the date, then appliqué the label to the quilt lining with blind stitch.

## Marie Shirer

*At the age of 3 while most of us were learning to recite the ABCs, Marie had already learned to sew. It's been an important part of her life since then. Marie made her first quilt while still in college. After graduation she owned and managed a quilting and needlework store in Kansas for nine years. In 1982, Marie joined the staff of Quilter's Newsletter Magazine, where she spent 12½ years as special projects editor and senior features editor. In 1995, Marie was named managing editor–New Products at Leman Publications. Christmas on Parade is the sixth book she has written. Marie loves celebrating Christmas with family and friends, but her favorite part is Christmas Eve when she gets to read the Nativity story at her church.*

*Marie Shirer (left) and Marla Stefanelli (right).*

## Marla Stefanelli

*Like Marie, Marla started doing needlework projects at the early age of 5, learning to sew, crochet, embroider and knit. She made her first quilt 20 years ago. In addition to sewing, drawing and painting are Marla's other passions. Working first as a costume designer and then joining the Leman Publications staff in 1982 as a graphic artist and quilt designer for Quilter's Newsletter Magazine and Quiltmaker, Marla has been able to combine her two talents: sewing and art. Over the years Marla has designed dozens of patterns, including her popular Continuous Line Quilting Design collections. She has also illustrated and drafted patterns for nine quilt books. Her favorite part of Christmas is making quilts and fabric crafts for her friends and family!*